Bearded
Dragons

THOMAS MAZORLIG

ANIMAL PLANET ♥ PET CARE LIBRARY

Bearded Dragons

Project Team
Editor: Stephanie Fornino
Indexer: Ann W. Truesdale
Design Concept: Leah Lococo Ltd.,
Stephanie Krautheim
Design Layout: Patricia Escabi

TFH Publications®
President/CEO: Glen S. Axelrod
Executive Vice President: Mark E. Johnson
Publisher: Christopher T. Reggio
Production Manager: Kathy Bontz

TFH Publications, Inc.®
One TFH Plaza
Third and Union Avenues
Neptune City, NJ 07753

Discovery Communications, LLC. Book Development Team: Marjorie Kaplan, President and General Manager, Animal Planet Media/ Kelly Day, Executive Vice President and General Manager, Discovery Commerce/ Elizabeth Bakacs, Vice President, Licensing and Creative/ JP Stoops, Director, Licensing/ Bridget Stoyko, Associate Art Director, Licensing

©2011 Discovery Communications, LLC. Animal Planet and the Animal Planet logo are trademarks of Discovery Communications, LLC, used under license. All rights reserved. animalplanet.com

Interior design, text, and photos ©2011 TFH Publications, Inc.

Printed and bound in China.
11 12 13 14 15   1 3 5 7 9 8 6 4 2

Library of Congress Cataloging-in-Publication Data
Mazorlig, Tom.
  Bearded dragons / Thomas Mazorlig.
    p. cm.
  Includes index.
  ISBN 978-0-7938-3713-7 (alk. paper)
  1. Bearded dragons (Reptiles) as pets. 2. Bearded dragons (Reptiles) I. Title.
  SF459.L5M287 2011
  639.3'955–dc22
                          2011003080

The Leader in Responsible Animal Care for Over 50 Years!®
www.tfh.com

Table of Contents

Chapter 1

Here, There Be

Dragons

If you want a lizard who's full of personality, easy to handle, and fun to watch, a bearded dragon may be the right one for you. Bearded dragons' spiky prehistoric appearance belies their sociable demeanor—they seem to enjoy interacting with people almost as much as the people enjoy interacting with them. On top of this, bearded dragons are hardy lizards and make good pets for those new to keeping pet reptiles. Do you think that you are ready to care for one of these energetic and interesting creatures? This book will help you answer that question and provide you with a complete look at what life is like when you live with a dragon.

What Is a Bearded Dragon?

Let's start with the basics. Bearded dragons, also affectionately known as "beardies," are lizards, and that makes them reptiles. To scientists, breeders, and savvy keepers, the bearded dragon we're concerned with in this book is known as the inland bearded dragon, with the official scientific name of *Pogona vitticeps*. There are other species of bearded dragons, and all are members of the genus (the level above species and below family) *Pogona*. The inland bearded dragon is the only bearded dragon species that is commonly kept as a pet, so unless otherwise stated, in this book "bearded dragon" always means this species.

Bearded dragons are medium-sized lizards; when fully grown, a bearded dragon will be from 16 to 24 inches (40.6 to 61 cm) from the snout to the tail. Males are bigger than females and are usually not smaller than 20 inches (50.8 cm). A little more than half a dragon's length is in his tail.

Bearded dragons are named for the pointy frill of skin under the chin. They can inflate this into a spiky beard that makes the lizard appear much larger. Beardies do this to ward off predators and territorial rivals and also as part of their courtship display. The beards of female dragons are less impressive than those of the males.

Range and Habitat

Bearded dragons are found over much of eastern Australia. They live in mostly hot and dry habitats, ranging from true deserts to scrubby forests. Beardies are excellent climbers and spend a lot of their time basking on tree limbs. They adapt well to human presence and will live in yards, gardens, and farms. They are often seen basking on fences.

The Expert Knows

All in the Family

Bearded dragons are members of the family Agamidae, and members of that family are called agamas or agamids. This is a very large family of lizards from the eastern hemisphere, with more than 300 species. Bearded dragons are by far the most popular pet lizards in this family, but green water dragons and uromastyx lizards also are fairly common pet agamas. The frilled lizard (*Chlamydosaurus kingii*) is the star of many nature programs because of the dramatic frill of skin these agamas can flare out when confronted with danger. Frilled lizards are becoming more popular in the pet trade. The largest agamas are the sailfin lizards (genus *Hydrosaurus*), from Indonesia and the Philippines. These semi-aquatic herbivorous lizards can reach lengths of 4 feet (1.2 m).

Bearded dragons are found naturally in the deserts and arid forests of central and eastern Australia.

Diet

Wild beardies are omnivores, feeding on a wide range of plants and animals. They eat mostly leaves, shoots, and flowers but also consume a significant amount of insects and other small animals. Pet bearded dragons also require a varied diet of vegetables, fruits, and insects.

Behavior and Body Language

Bearded dragons have a number of interesting—sometimes amusing— behaviors that you're likely to see if you have one as a pet. Most of these behaviors are connected to the lizard's territorial nature or to its courtship. Even if you are keeping only one beardie, he may display at his reflection, at other household pets, or just because.

Arm Waving

Arm waving is a curious behavior that you probably won't see unless you have multiple bearded dragons. It's a social behavior and seems to be a way of signaling to a dominant male bearded dragon that the arm-waving lizard poses no threat. It is performed mostly by juveniles and females.

When a beardie performs arm waving, he will stand tall on his two hind legs and one foreleg. He will extend the other foreleg out and move it slowly in a wide circle. The arm moves back to front. If you have a group of hatchlings together, when one starts arm-waving, the rest often follow suit. This makes it look like some bizarre bearded dragon version of synchronized swimming, or as a friend once put it, signaling the mother ship.

This dragon is inflating his beard in a threatening or territorial display.

Eye Bulging

Eye bulging is a bizarre behavior, and no one is quite sure why bearded dragons do it. It looks almost exactly as you think it would: the eyes swell up and protrude. It can last a while, so don't be alarmed unless your dragon's eyes haven't returned to normal after an hour.

Head Bobbing

Head bobbing is a way for a male dragon to announce that he's the ruler of his little patch of territory. It's how he advertises his virility. A male dragon performs head bobbing when another beardie enters his territory or if he is trying to court a female. Head bobbing looks as if the dragon is doing pushups, and his beard darkens to a black or bluish black at the same time. A head-bobbing male often sits in a prominent position such as a branch or tall rock.

Inflating the Beard

The bearded dragon's most famous attribute is the beard. This is a pouch of extensible skin covered in pointy scales. A dragon will inflate his beard when he is angry, trying to scare off a predator, or fighting off a territorial rival. When he inflates his beard, it will turn a deep black or bluish black color and will appear like a spiky shield. It makes the bearded dragon's head seem much larger. Usually combined with a gaping mouth—revealing the bright yellow interior—and some hissing, this makes an impressive display. Males are more prone to this behavior, but females do it too, although a female's beard is smaller than and not as dark as a male's. If your dragon is inflating his beard, it is probably a good idea to avoid handling him at that moment. He is highly agitated and may bite.

Life Span

Pet bearded dragons given excellent care normally live from 9 to 12 years, although there are dragons who occasionally live longer than 12 years. Unfortunately, many don't live this long, and it is usually due to some failing of the keeper to provide for his needs. Before you acquire one, be certain that you are willing to provide him excellent care for at least a decade.

arm or in your lap while you watch TV or surf the web. Yet they don't seem to mind if you don't have time to handle them for a day or two—as long as you are still providing otherwise excellent care. They do not need to be taken out for walks, and they do not trigger allergies. Bearded dragons are noise-free and almost odor-free pets.

Beardies make very hardy pets—they are adaptable and not prone to many illnesses. The illnesses they do get result mostly from improper care. While they do have specific requirements, their needs are not too exacting for a first-time lizard keeper. In fact, they are one of the best lizards for someone who has never had a pet lizard before.

Bearded Dragons as Pets

Bearded dragons have a number of attributes that have made them one of the most popular pet lizards. However, they are not the pet for everyone. Like other pets, they have their particular needs, and it is the responsibility of the pet owner to meet those needs.

The Good

Bearded dragons are personable lizards who seem to actually enjoy being handled. They are rarely aggressive and almost never bite. They are usually content to sit on your

If you want a pet lizard you can handle, a bearded dragon is one of the best choices. They are very tolerant of gentle handling.

Herp Is the Word

A word used in this book that may be new to you is "herp." This is the term for all reptiles and amphibians collectively. It comes from "herpetology," which is the study of reptiles and amphibians, and that term is derived from the Greek word herpeton, meaning "creeping thing." The people who keep herps as a hobby are usually called "herpers" or "herp hobbyists." Breeding herps in captivity is often called "herpetoculture." You'll see these terms a lot as you do more research on bearded dragons or on herps in general.

The Bad

There are no more or fewer difficulties in keeping a beardie than there are in keeping cats, dogs, or other pets; the difficulties are just different ones. One of the major issues for some people is that bearded dragons require live insects as food. You will need to buy (and care for) crickets, mealworms, and possibly some other insects to provide food for your lizard. Putting together a proper dragon diet may seem a bit complicated, because unlike dogs or cats, these lizards don't eat kibble out of a bag.

Bearded dragons are creatures of the Australian Outback. One will not be comfortable—and indeed won't survive—unless you bring a little of the Outback into his cage. You'll need to provide heat, specialized lighting, and some cage furnishings to create a suitable habitat for your scaly friend. And that cage won't be small. Beardies are good-sized, active lizards. An adult needs an enclosure at least the size of a 55-gallon (208.2-l) tank—something roughly 4 feet (1.2 m) long.

Making the Decision

At this point, you may think that a bearded dragon sounds like the pet for you, but you aren't totally sure. Read the rest of this book and think objectively about whether or not you are willing and able to provide the care one needs. Think about the physical space and time in your schedule you will have to dedicate to this pet. Don't forget you also have to discuss this subject with your family and/or housemates. Even if you are the only one caring for the lizard, they will be sharing the house with him.

Once you have done your research and thought it over carefully, you may or may not decide that a bearded dragon is the right pet for you. If you are going to get one, start gathering the supplies and tracking down sources of bearded dragons. If not, you can start looking for a pet that is better suited to your situation.

A bearded dragon needs some live insects in his diet, something to consider before you get one.

Where to Get a Bearded Dragon

If you've decided that a bearded dragon is the pet for you, your next question is probably going to be "Where do I get one?" There are several places where you can find a bearded bundle of joy to bring home. There are pet stores, herp shows, online sellers, and animal shelters and reptile rescues.

Pet Stores

Pet stores probably are the most common source of bearded dragons. Almost any pet store that stocks reptiles will have beardies, although these lizards may be scarcer in the winter and early spring. Normally, pet stores sell dragons who are about two to four months old. The benefits of buying from a pet store are that it will sell most of the supplies you need, you can examine the beardies closely, you can see them feed, and there is probably a store located close by. Also, many pet stores have a health guarantee on their livestock.

You will probably have several dragons from which to choose. Before zeroing in on that one beardie who's meant for you, take a look at all of the dragons in the cage. They should all be in good condition, in a clean cage, with food and water. The cage should not be overcrowded. If you don't like the way the dragons—or any of the other animals—are being kept, seek out another source. There's no reason to reward a shoddy pet store with your money.

If you feel good about the shop and its bearded dragons, go for a closer look. The dragons should be alert and

Bearded dragons are available in several color varieties, such as this orange phase dragon.

notice your presence. Most beardies are not very afraid of people, so carefully scooping one up for an inspection shouldn't be difficult. Even if the dragons run away from you, don't be concerned, because most beardies tame easily. Once in your hand, the beardie should be checked for any signs of poor health: discharge from the eyes or nostrils, feces smeared around or stuck to the vent (the slit under the tail for expelling waste), listlessness, dragging a limb, being too skinny, or any odd swellings or discolorations. Also, check for mites. (See Chapter 5.) If he passes muster, you can pay the clerk and take your dragon home.

Herp Shows

Herp shows (also called herp expos, reptile shows, and reptile expos) are gatherings of people interested in reptiles and amphibians. They are usually held at fairgrounds, sports stadiums, and convention centers, and they occur every few months in most of the lower 48 states. At a herp expo you will find breeders, wholesale animal dealers, booksellers, supply vendors, and anyone else who has a herp-related or herp-themed product to sell. Bearded dragons are sure to be present at any herp expo, often ranging from hatchlings to adults. (Adults are usually retired breeders; one would make a great pet, although he may be quite old when you purchase him.) A herp show is a great place to get a specific color variety of bearded dragon, if that's what you want.

At a herp show, your best bet is to buy directly from one of the breeders. They will be very knowledgeable about their particular lizards and often have good prices. There should be several, and you can compare the prices, ages, colors, and other qualities. When you are narrowing down your choices, inspect the dragons for health, just as you would at a pet store. This is also a good time to ask any questions you might have regarding the breeder's dragons or just bearded dragon care in general. But be reasonable—these shows can be busy, and the breeder may have several customers at his or her table.

The biggest drawback to buying a bearded dragon at a show is that there is usually no guarantee on the animal's health. The better breeders will provide you with contact information and might offer some type of guarantee, but don't count on this.

Online Sellers

You can buy bearded dragons over the Internet. Searching for "bearded dragon breeders" will turn up numerous hits. This is probably the best way to buy a bearded dragon if you are looking for a specific color variety or wish to buy a dragon from a nationally known breeder who is not situated near you. Many breeders will have pictures of each dragon they have for sale, and you can select the exact one you want.

There are some drawbacks to buying dragons online. For one, you can't inspect them at all. This means

Unless you have an enormous enclosure, you should only keep one dragon per cage. These are territorial lizards.

to avoid). The last drawback to online buying is the cost of shipping. The cost of having a live animal shipped overnight can be pretty high.

Animal Shelters and Reptile Rescues

As bearded dragons have grown in popularity, so has the number of unwanted beardies who end up at animal shelters and reptile rescues. These places can be great sources for a pet beardie. However, many of their animals have been neglected by their previous owners and may have health problems. They may also require some taming. If you want to give an unfortunate beardie a good home, check your local animal shelter and see whether it has bearded dragons currently or ever gets them. If not, the staff may know of a local reptile rescue that may have beardies. You can also search for reptile rescues and bearded dragon rescues online.

Males and Females

Many people considering a pet bearded dragon wonder if they should get a male or a female. This then leads them to wonder how to tell a male dragon from a female.

How to Tell the Difference

It is very difficult to determine the sex of a young bearded dragon. There are no reliable visible differences between male and female dragons until they reach about three months of age. At that time, the differences become apparent and grow more distinct as the

Should I Have More Than One?

Bearded dragons are not social creatures. In fact, they are rather territorial and often resent the presence of others, and this is especially true of males. So your beardie will not be lonely if he doesn't have another dragon to play with. Chances are he will be happier that way.

If you really want to have a pair or a few beardies, plan to house each one in his own cage. While keepers do successfully house beardies in groups, this works only if the enclosure is very large. It also works only if there is just one male present, and even that is risky if the male is kept with a female or females. Males have been known to attack and even kill females. It really is best to give everyone his or her own enclosure.

that you have to take the seller's word for it that the dragons are healthy. Most online vendors only guarantee live arrival. That is, once the dragon is out of the shipping box and in your home, any problems are your responsibility. One way to avoid problems is to ask around on the various reptile forums for recommended breeders (and those

Place your dragon in his enclosure as soon as possible after bringing him home.

dragon ages. Adult bearded dragons are pretty easy to sex once you know what to look for.

Male dragons are generally larger and more robust than females and usually have larger and darker beards. If you look at the base of the underside of the tail, the male's is usually much thicker than the female's. Additionally, adult males have visible pores on the underside of the thigh. These secrete a waxy substance used for territory marking. It's important to look at a number of these characteristics because there is a lot of variation among dragons. For example, some female dragons have prominent beards.

There is another method to tell male dragons from females, and it is very exact once you know how to do it. Place the dragon on a flat surface. Use one hand to gently hold him in place. Using the other hand, lift the tail up until it makes a nearly 90-degree angle with the body. Do this gently so that you don't injure his tail. Now look at the base of the tail near the vent. If there are two long oval swellings below the vent—one on each side of the tail—with a little dip or gully between them, the dragon is a male. If instead there is a roughly triangular bump just behind the vent, the dragon is female.

Which One Makes the Best Pet?

If you don't plan to breed your dragon, his or her gender will not make much difference to your keeping experience. Males can be more rambunctious and less tame, but they almost always become friendly pets.

FAMILY-FRIENDLY TIP

Are Bearded Dragons Good Pets for Kids?

Quite often, it's one of the children in the family who really wants a pet bearded dragon. That's fine, but in reality it is always best for the lizard if one or more adults are in charge of his care. A kid may really want a beardie, but that interest may wane when summer comes or when soccer practice starts. Also, most children haven't developed the sense of responsibility it takes to perform the day-to-day care a bearded dragon requires—of course, being partially responsible for some of the care can help teach responsibility. So even if you are getting a bearded dragon for your kid, you have to be the one who makes sure that the lizard is getting the care he needs.

They will engage in territorial displays and can be somewhat aggressive at these times. Females tend to be more docile. However, females can produce eggs even without a male present, creating the risk of life-threatening egg binding. (See Chapter 5 details.) Males obviously never become egg bound. The differences between the sexes are minor, and both males and females make wonderful pets.

Bringing Home a Dragon

If you obtain your beardie from a local source, you will need to transport him home. The best way to do so is in a cooler. A cooler is nicely insulated from any temperature extremes. Additionally, the darkness will keep your lizard calm. If you don't have a cooler, any big-enough box will do. On a cold day, you can line it with towels to hold in the warmth.

Your dragon will be sold to you in some type of small container, which could be a lidded plastic container, a small box, or a cloth bag. Baby dragons are often sold in deli cups. Place this inside the cooler and use towels as padding around the container holding the dragon, being careful not to cover its air holes.

Assuming that you're using a car for transport, you may need the heat on in the car or even the air-conditioning, depending on the temperature. On a cold day, you should have the car warmed up before bringing your dragon out to it. Minimize his exposure to the winter's chill as much as you can. In the summer, keep the cooler out of direct sunlight. Never direct the car's air-conditioning vents to blow hot or cold air directly onto the container no matter what the temperature outside.

You should drive straight home, making no unnecessary stops. When you get home, unpack your beardie carefully and put him into his enclosure as quickly as possible. Give him at least day to settle in before you start handling him. He's had a stressful move and will need a bit of time to get used to his new family and the unfamiliar surroundings.

The Other Bearded Dragons

The inland bearded dragon is the most common species of bearded dragon in the pet trade, but it is not the only one. There are two others that are occasionally available: the eastern bearded dragon (*Pogona barbata*) and Lawson's dragon (*Pogona henrylawsoni*). Both of these lizards are similar to the common beardie, but there are some important differences.

The eastern bearded dragon looks enough like the inland species that the two can be confused. Easterns tend to be darker in color, and the males have the largest beards of all of the species. They can grow a bit larger than inland dragons, but the size range of the two species overlaps. Eastern dragons—originally residents of coastal Australia—are better able to withstand cool and moist conditions than the other species.

Lawson's dragon is sold under several names, including Rankin's dragon, dwarf bearded dragon, and black soil bearded dragon. It is much smaller than the inland dragon, only reaching a length of 10 to 12 inches (25.4 to 30.5 cm). Lawson's dragon has a very small, almost vestigial beard. This species is more sensitive to low temperatures and high humidity than the inland dragon.

While both of these lizards make rewarding pets, it is best for a beginning keeper to start with the common inland bearded dragon. There is more readily available information for the inland dragon, which is helpful to new hobbyists. Additionally, the inland is hardier and easier to handle.

Hatchling Lawson's Dragon

Chapter 2

A Dragon's Lair and

What's Inside

Like most other pets, bearded dragons need a certain amount of equipment to keep them successfully. The most important thing a beardie needs is a cage or other suitable enclosure. Inside this enclosure, you will be creating a simulation of his natural habitat: the Australian desert. Because of this, you'll need to consider heating and lighting options. There are a few other items he'll need as well.

Glass aquaria are the most common enclosures for bearded dragons.

The Enclosure

A bearded dragon's enclosure is his home within your home. It is here where he will spend most of his time. There are several options for bearded dragon enclosures.

Types of Enclosures

The two most common types of dragon enclosures are glass aquaria and molded plastic cages. Both are readily available and easy to set up. There are several other options that may also be worth considering depending on your circumstances.

Glass Aquaria

By far the most common enclosure used for bearded dragons is the glass aquarium. These are readily available in a range of sizes, and they offer excellent visibility. Glass holds heat nicely, so heating aquaria is generally not an issue. Because they come in set sizes, it usually isn't a problem to find a screen lid and a stand that will fit your aquarium. If you have a particularly large aquarium or one that is of a less common size or shape, you may need to special order the stand and lid.

Glass aquaria do have their disadvantages. At the size needed for a beardie, a glass aquarium is going to be very heavy. The weight can make it difficult to clean because moving it to a place where cleaning is easy (such as out on a patio) may be impossible. Glass is also breakable. Drop the water bowl onto it once and you may need to shop for a new enclosure—immediately.

There are now glass enclosures made just for reptiles. They look much like a regular glass aquarium. They are of slightly thinner glass, so they are more lightweight than a normal aquarium. Most come with a locking screen top that slides on a track. They are normally a bit less expensive than buying a glass aquarium and screen top separately.

Molded Plastic Cages

Another type of enclosure suitable for bearded dragons is the molded plastic cage. There are several different brands, and these cages are made specifically for use with reptiles. The sides, bottom, and usually the top are opaque, with a sliding glass or acrylic door on the front. The sliding door makes cleaning and accessing the cage easier, although it is also easier for your dragon to bolt out through when it's opened. Most brands have several recessed areas in the top to accommodate lights. They are very lightweight and durable. The biggest disadvantage is the cost; they are much more expensive than aquaria. Also, most pet stores do not carry these cages, although your local pet store may be able to order one for you. You might need to order one through an online vendor or buy one at a herp show. Some models may not have good ventilation.

Other Types

There are a few other types of enclosures that are used less commonly for bearded dragons. One is a cattle watering trough. These are large metal or plastic containers that are used much as their name suggests—for providing water to livestock. These large containers are mostly used by breeders and hobbyists with a large collection of dragons. Each one can generally house a trio of beardies. They are deep enough that they do not need a lid, provided there are no other pets, such as cats or dogs, who could get into the trough and harm your dragon. Additionally, you have to be careful when arranging the cage furnishings;

Cage Before Dragon

You should have your dragon's home all set up and ready for several days before you bring him home. There are two reasons for this. One is that you don't want your new friend to be stuck in a box or bag while you scramble to get everything set up. This will cause him unnecessary stress, and during this time he will likely be too cold. The other reason is that by having the cage set up ahead of time, you can monitor the temperatures and make sure that they are in the appropriate range. If there is some problem with the heating devices, it's much better to know before your dragon is in the enclosure and subjected to being terribly over- or underheated.

Bearded Dragons

they must not be so high that a bearded dragon could use them to climb or leap out of the cage. Considering their great size and durability, these enclosures are fairly inexpensive.

Similar to the cattle watering trough, one of the larger tortoise tubs on the market could be used as a bearded dragon enclosure. These containers are made of durable plastic. Most of them aren't deep enough to house a bearded dragon, but some of the larger models are. They will usually require a screen top to keep your dragon inside. Tortoise tubs may be one of the more expensive options for bearded dragon housing.

Acrylic aquaria are generally unsuitable as bearded dragon enclosures. Although they are lightweight and not prone to breaking, they scratch easily. A beardie's claws and a sand substrate will scratch the acrylic, making it unsightly and reducing visibility. Some cleaning products will also scratch or discolor acrylic. Acrylic aquaria are more expensive than traditional glass aquaria.

Enclosure Size

Bearded dragons are medium-sized, highly active lizards who like to move around their cages. To accommodate

Building Your Own

Some dragon keepers build their own enclosures. There is no reason not to do this if you have the know-how. Generally, building a custom enclosure is less expensive than buying one and allows you to have the exact enclosure you want. If this interests you, there are many resources available online—searching under "custom bearded dragon cages" turned up more than 250,000 results.

their active nature, an enclosure for one of these lizards must be fairly large. Additionally, the cage must be large enough to create a proper thermal gradient. (See section "Heating" below.) The minimum size aquarium for an adult is a 55-gallon (208-l) enclosure. If using some other type of enclosure, the minimum dimensions for the floor should be 3 feet by 2 feet (91.4 cm by 61 cm). If you are housing two bearded dragons together, you will need almost double that—12 square feet (365.8 cm) instead of the 6 square feet (182.9 cm) of floor area that the 3 feet by 2 feet (91.4 cm by 61 cm) enclosure provides.

Hatchlings require smaller housing. It is difficult for a hatchling to find his feeder insects if there is too much space. A hatchling or two will be quite comfortable in a 10- or 20-gallon (38- or 76-l) aquarium. Plan to move your hatchling to a larger enclosure by the time he is six months old.

While beardies enjoy climbing, they do not need height as much as they need floor space. An enclosure does not need to be any taller than your bearded dragon is long and can even be shorter than this. For an adult, about 15 inches (38 cm) is the suggested minimum height.

Placing the Enclosure

Give some careful thought to where you are going to place your beardie's enclosure. You want to make sure that there is enough room for both the cage and for you to maneuver around it when it needs to be cleaned.

Place your dragon's enclosure in an easily accessible area that is not exposed to drafts or to direct sunlight.

Place the cage in an area that will not receive direct sunlight. Although bearded dragons like it hot, direct sunlight could cause the inside of the enclosure to overheat dramatically and injure or even kill your pet. This is especially true with glass aquaria and molded plastic cages—they will act like a greenhouse when put in direct sunlight. Similarly, do not place the enclosure in a drafty spot. This will make it much harder to keep it properly heated.

Think about the traffic in the room in which you plan to put the enclosure. Bearded dragons are not shy creatures and are curious about their surroundings. Although you don't want to put yours someplace where there are people all the time and lots of noise, your beardie will enjoy seeing his humans come and go. A family room, den, or home office is probably ideal. Putting the cage in the kitchen is not recommended. The fumes from cooking and cleaning can possibly harm your dragon, and you want to keep him and all of his cage materials away from food preparation areas for hygiene reasons.

Security

Unlike some other reptiles, such as snakes, bearded dragons are not accomplished escape artists. Usually a simple screen lid on an aquarium or sliding door on a reptile cage will keep them inside their enclosure. If you are using some type of open-topped enclosure, make sure that none of the climbing branches reach high enough for your beardie to use to boost himself out. Also, make sure that he cannot scale the walls of the enclosure itself.

The other side of the security coin is keeping unwanted intruders, such as humans and other animals, out of your dragon's cage. If you have cats or dogs, a screen top should keep them out of a glass aquarium, although some cats will lie on top of the screen. (Hey, it's warm and there's entertainment below!) While this will stress your dragon initially, he is likely to adapt and learn to ignore the cat. Avoid using any type of open-topped enclosure if you have other household pets unless you can keep them out of the room containing your beardie's enclosure.

It is more difficult to keep other people out of the enclosure. Specifically, kids often want to handle bearded dragons a lot or take them out to show off to their friends. It's important to teach your child to handle the beardie only when an adult is there to supervise. It's also a good idea to have some type of lock on the cage opening as a back-up plan. Molded plastic cages and reptile-specific enclosures often come with locking doors.

Substrate

The substrate is the material that goes on the bottom of the cage. Although this is sometimes called bedding, it isn't used for bedding by bearded dragons the way that it is used by rodents. The function of the substrate is to absorb wastes for later cleanup and to give a bearded dragon some traction. If there were no substrate, the smooth floor of the enclosure would cause your beardie to slip around and not be able to walk in a natural fashion. Reptiles kept on smooth-bottomed enclosures over the long term may develop an abnormal gait.

Substrates are a controversial topic in the herp community. There are varying opinions on which ones are safe or unsafe and appropriate or inappropriate for different species. Some experts favor the most

This group of hatchlings is housed on newspaper, one of the safest and least expensive substrates for a dragon enclosure.

naturalistic substrates, while others prefer a more bare-bones approach. In the end, each individual keeper must learn all that he can on the subject and make an informed choice while keeping the best interests of the pet in mind.

Unsafe Choices

There are numerous substrates that are unsafe for bearded dragons, so we'll rule them out first and then discuss the pros and cons of the other substrates. Unsafe dragon substrates include gravel, wood shavings (such as the cedar and pine shavings intended for rodents), potting soil, crushed walnut shells, corncob bedding, bark substrates (such as mulch and products sold as "reptile

Leave the Artificial Turf Outside

Although some keepers confuse it with cage liners, artificial turf (e.g., indoor/outdoor carpeting, Astroturf) is not the same thing. Artificial turf is not designed for use in herp cages. The surface is made of thousands of tiny pieces of plastic, and these pieces break off over time, posing a choking and impaction risk. Also, the threads holding the carpeting together tend to fray. These threads can easily become wrapped around a toe or tail or even the neck. Artificial turf is completely unsafe for use in reptile enclosures.

bark"), kitty litter, and alfalfa pellets (and other variations, such as rabbit pellets). These substrates have a good chance of causing gut impaction when ingested. They literally block up the digestive tract and prevent the passage of food. This condition is fatal if not treated by a veterinarian right away.

Calcium-based sand is another potentially unsafe substrate. It is sold in pet store reptile departments under several brand names. Although it seems that sand made from calcium would be beneficial, it can be an impaction risk.

Some of the other unsafe substrates are inappropriate for bearded dragons for other reasons besides being impaction risks. Many wood shavings contain volatile oils that may irritate a beardie's skin and mucous membranes. There is some anecdotal evidence they cause liver damage, but there have been no conclusive studies. Alfalfa pellets are a lower impaction risk than some of the other substrates, although they have been implicated in some cases of impaction. The other danger of these pellets is that when they become wet (such as when your dragon defecates) they are easily colonized by bacteria and fungi. Because beardies often like the taste, they are likely to eat the pathogen-laden pellets and then possibly become sick.

Safe Choices

Now that you know what substrates not to use, you are probably wondering "Well, what the heck is safe to use?" There are several options, and each has its own benefits and drawbacks.

Cage Liners

Reptile cage liners are available at most pet stores and online. When buying cage liners, purchase those specifically made for use in reptile cages, and make sure that there are no little loops of thread that could catch a toe. Cage liners are cut to fit standard-sized tanks, so you may have to use several to cover the floor space if you have a very large or custom-made enclosure.

It's very helpful to have extra cage liners on hand. They will allow you to immediately replace a dirty one. Replacing the liners is easy, and you can clean them by throwing them into the washing machine or washing them in a tub or sink. Use hot water to help kill bacteria unless the manufacturer's label specifically says not to do so. A benefit of cage liners is that they are thin, so they allow the heat from undertank heating devices to penetrate easily.

One drawback to cage liners is that bearded dragons cannot perform normal digging and burrowing behaviors. You also cannot spot clean the liners. If one spot is dirty, the whole thing must be cleaned. Some keepers find the look of cage liners unnatural or unsightly, while others like it.

Newspaper

One of the cheapest substrates around is newspaper. Numerous keepers have successfully used newspaper with bearded dragons and other reptiles for decades. It may be the safest of all the substrates, posing no risk of impaction. Some keepers express concern about the ink, although there is no evidence it causes harm. If you share this concern, you can use unprinted newsprint, which is available at any store that sells arts and crafts supplies. When using newspaper, do not use any glossy pieces. They may contain harmful ingredients and at the very least will not absorb wastes at all.

As with cage liners, when the newspaper is soiled you must remove the whole piece and dispose of it, then replace it with new pieces. (Note that newspaper, along with dragon droppings, is compostable.) You can easily cut pieces to fit your enclosure exactly. Newspaper isn't terribly absorbent, so dragons may walk through their droppings, resulting in

Many keepers use sand as the substrate in their bearded dragon enclosures. Child's play sand is the safest for use with these lizards.

Although not commonly used as a substrate for bearded dragons, recycled paper bedding works well for this purpose.

smearing that you will need to clean. Bearded dragons cannot dig or burrow in newspaper, although many discover that they can pull it up and crawl underneath. Feeder insects often hide beneath the newspaper as well; be careful of this or crickets may come out later and attack your beardie. (See Chapter 3 for more on this subject.)

Newspaper works best when placed in the cage in a few layers. Make sure that the pieces fit the cage well. Places where it rides up the wall will give feeder insects an easy place to slip beneath it. Newspaper is one of the best substrates for housing hatchlings.

Play Sand

Sand sold for playgrounds and children's sandboxes makes a good substrate for beardies. Note that this is not the same as the sand sold at pet stores specifically for reptiles. Because of impaction risks, most of those sands are actually not recommended. Play sand does pose some risk of impaction, although many breeders and hobbyists have used this substrate for years without a problem. If you wish to use sand but fear impaction, always feed your bearded dragon in a separate container. This will prevent him from ingesting the sand when he eats.

Play sand is found at toy, hardware, and home and garden stores. The sand makes the enclosure heavy, especially if you are using it in a large enclosure, and it creates a natural desert appearance. It also holds heat well and allows beardies to dig and burrow to their heart's content. You can do some spot cleaning with play sand so that you don't have to change the whole substrate too frequently.

When using a sand substrate, cover the bottom of the enclosure to a depth of at least 3 inches (7.6 cm) to allow your lizard to burrow. Undertank heating pads will not be able to penetrate sand very well. Additionally, a dragon who burrows under the sand above an undertank heater may become overheated or burn. Using these devices with a sand substrate is not recommended.

Recycled Paper Bedding

Recycled paper bedding is a substrate normally used for rodents. It actually makes an excellent substrate for bearded dragons, along with numerous other reptile species. You can find it in the small animal section of most pet stores. This product is a by-product of newspaper manufacture. The manufacturers claim that it is completely safe for herps and will pass through their digestive tract without causing impaction. It is absorbent, lightweight, and soft. Bearded dragons can burrow into recycled paper bedding easily. It can be spot cleaned and is both flushable and compostable.

The drawbacks to recycled paper bedding are the cost, the appearance, and the odor. Recycled paper bedding is one of the more expensive substrates for beardies. This substrate does not appear natural and is a fairly unattractive gray color. (There is a white variety available too, but to some that looks even more bizarre.) Some keepers find the smell of this substrate unpleasant, but others just find it a bit earthy. A more minor disadvantage is that it can be difficult to see droppings on this material.

Cover the bottom of the enclosure with about 3 inches (7.6 cm) of recycled paper bedding. If you are using this as a substrate for hatchlings, use a much thinner layer, less than 1 inch (2.5 cm). I used recycled paper bedding in all of my bearded dragon enclosures and found it to be an excellent—if somewhat expensive—substrate. Some breeders have said that this product seemed to promote dehydration in hatchlings. I never found this to be the case, but it is something to be aware of if you are keeping hatchlings on it.

The Expert Knows

Be Accurate

Don't guess how warm it is in your beardie's cage. Use an accurate thermometer to keep track of the temperatures. It's best to have a thermometer measuring the basking spot temperature and another measuring the cool end. If the cage is too hot or too cold, your lizard's health will suffer.

In nature, bearded dragons regulate their body temperature by moving into sunlight to warm up and into the shade to cool off.

Other Paper Substrates

Plain brown paper towels and butcher paper can also be used as substrates. These have most of the same pros and cons as newspaper. They are somewhat more expensive than newspaper. Paper toweling is the most absorbent of the three.

Heating

Bearded dragons live in deserts, so it should come as no surprise that they need to be kept warm. What may be surprising is that they actually need a range of temperatures and temperature fluctuations between daytime and nighttime to remain healthy and happy.

Behavioral Thermoregulation

Unlike mammals, reptiles produce very little of their own body heat, instead relying on the environment to provide the warmth they need for their metabolism. This is why reptiles and amphibians are often called "cold-blooded" animals. A more accurate term would be "ectothermic"; *ecto-* means "outside" and *–thermic* means "relating to heat," so the term means "heat from outside."

The ultimate source of a bearded dragon's heat is the sun. For a dragon to warm himself, he'll move into the sunlight. When he has reached a temperature that is warm enough for him to become active, he'll move out of the sun and start foraging, looking for mates, defending his territory, and engaging in other activities. If it becomes too warm for him, a dragon will move into the shade or burrow under a rock or stump to cool down. By using areas in his habitat that vary in temperature, a bearded dragon can keep his temperature within a preferred range. The term "behavioral thermoregulation" refers to reptiles' use of their behavior to control body temperature.

What all of this means for the keeper is that a bearded dragon cannot be kept at one set temperature. He needs a range of temperatures so that he can raise or lower his own temperature as needed. You will have to provide this temperature range (called a thermal gradient) within his enclosure. But this is not as difficult as you might fear.

Creating a Temperature Range

The easiest way to create the proper thermal gradient is to keep all of the heating devices—usually a heat lamp or two—at one end of the cage and leave the other end unheated. This will naturally create a warm end on one side of the enclosure and a cooler end on the other. Your bearded dragon can then move from one end to the other to regulate his temperature as needed.

During the day, the cool end of your dragon's enclosure should be 80°F (26.7°C) or a bit lower. That may not sound cool to a person, but it's cool for a bearded dragon. The hottest spot of the cage—the basking spot directly beneath a heat lamp—should range between 100° and 110°F (37.8° and 43.3°C). If you have a hatchling, the basking spot should be at the high end of that range; adult dragons are fine with basking sites at the low end of that range.

Deserts cool off dramatically at night, so your beardie is adapted to a nightly temperature drop. If the temperature in your house doesn't go below 65°F (18.3°C) at night, you won't need to provide any additional heating. If it gets cooler than that at night, you will need supplemental nighttime heating. A ceramic heat emitter (see section below) is perfect for this job.

Thermometers

You must be sure that your lizard's cage is the proper temperature at all times. To do this, you will need an accurate thermometer. You should actually use two: one for the warm end of the cage and one for the cool end.

Most pet stores carry several types of thermometers. The thin plastic strips that stick on the side of a glass aquarium are not recommended; they

Bearded dragons need to have a basking site that reaches 100° to 110°F (37.8° to 43.3°C).

Hot Rocks Are Not So Hot

One heating device that you should not use in a bearded dragon enclosure (or probably any other herp enclosure) is the hot rock (heat rock, sizzle stone, etc.). These are heating coils surrounded by some type of resin and shaped and colored to resemble a stone. When plugged in, they heat up. Although the new models are much better than the ones from the past, these items are still problematic. They heat up only a small spot of the cage, not the actual air temperature. This forces a bearded dragon to stay on the stone if he wants to be warm. Additionally, they can have spots where the resin is thinner than others, resulting in a spot that could be dangerously hot. These items have caused very serious burns in reptiles. It is much safer for your bearded dragon if you heat his cage with a heat lamp.

thermometers run off a battery and have an external probe that you can run into the cage at the exact spot you want to measure the temperature. Most of these thermometers have the capacity to record the lowest and highest temperatures in a 24-hour period, a handy feature for knowing exactly how hot and how cold the enclosure gets on a normal day. You can find these thermometers at department stores, electronics stores, and hardware stores. Additionally, more pet stores are starting to carry them.

Another thermometer highly recommended by many reptile breeders is an infrared temperature gun. This high-tech device records the temperature at a distant place when pointed at it. Infrared temperature guns are highly accurate. They are especially useful if you have multiple cages—you can just point the gun at each cage in turn and see what the temperature is at a glance. Temperature guns also let you see the temperature at multiple spots in a cage in just a few seconds, without having to move a thermometer around and waiting for it to register. The best places to buy a temperature gun are at herp expos and from online vendors.

Heating Equipment

A number of different heating devices exist that are suitable for heating bearded dragon enclosures. The most common and highly recommended are heat lamps, undertank heaters, and ceramic heat emitters. Heat tape was formerly a common method for heating reptile enclosures, but it can be tricky

can be wildly inaccurate. The stick-on thermometers that have a needle gauge are better but still not the best.

One of the best options is a digital thermometer. These very accurate to use safely and is not suitable for bearded dragons.

Heat Lamps

In nature, bearded dragons spend much of their time basking in the sunlight. This makes heat lamps a particularly suitable way to heat your beardie's enclosure. A nice bright heat lamp will create a basking spot that your bearded dragon will use frequently.

In their most common form, heat lamps consist of a socket with a reflective metal dome. They can rest on the screen cage top or be suspended above the cage in some fashion. Some heat lamps come with a clamp so that they can be attached to a light stand or something similar.

The bulb that you use in your dragon's heat lamp should be bright white or yellow, not red. You can use the bulbs sold at pet stores specifically for use with reptiles, regular household bulbs, floodlights, or spotlights. As long as the bulb is bright and produces enough heat, it should be fine for your dragon.

Place the light at one end of the cage. It's a good idea to put a flat rock (such as a piece of slate) on the bottom of the cage directly beneath the light. The light will heat up the rock and create a toasty spot for your dragon. The rock will stay fairly warm at night, enabling your beardie to warm himself if he feels the need. Another option is to angle a climbing branch so that it gets close to the light—but not so close that your beardie can burn himself.

Bearded dragons bask on branches in the wild, so by positioning one in this manner you are creating a natural habitat feature that he will use.

Undertank Heaters

Undertank heaters are specifically made for heating the enclosures of reptiles and amphibians. They are thin pads with a heating coil inside that get warm when plugged in. One side is coated with adhesive

Basking beardies often hold their mouths partially open, a behavior that may be similar to a dog's panting.

so that the heater sticks to the bottom of the enclosure. Most of these heaters are made to go on the bottom of glass aquariums and should not be used on other types of enclosures.

Undertank heaters are useful for making sure that the basking site reaches a high enough temperature, but for most keepers, basking lights alone should be enough. If you do use an undertank heater, shut it off at night along with the lights. If your house gets too cold at night for your dragon to be without heat, you can use an undertank heater as a nighttime heat source. However, you must be cautious when doing this. Bearded dragons will sometimes stay on a heater at night even if it is too hot for them. To prevent your dragon from being burned, make sure that the temperature directly above the undertank heater is not too hot for him—it only needs to keep him from getting colder than 65°F (18.3°C) or so.

Ceramic Heat Emitters

One way to think about ceramic heat emitters is that they are lightbulbs that give off heat instead of light. While not quite accurate, this definition does sum up their function. Ceramic heat emitters are made of ceramic surrounding a heating coil and an end that screws into a light socket. When you turn them on, they generate a lot of heat. They are excellent for nighttime heating because they generate no light that would disturb your dragon's— or your own—sleep cycle. If you do need to heat your beardie's enclosure at night, a ceramic heat emitter is probably your best option.

The biggest drawback to heat emitters is that they generate so much heat that they cannot safely be used

Along with a heat lamp, bearded dragons also need a bulb that provides them with ultraviolet light.

in a regular light socket; they will melt plastic and possibly start a fire. You will need to purchase a ceramic socket, one that doesn't have an on/off switch. (These on/off switches are made of plastic and will eventually malfunction.) This does mean that the only way to turn them off is to unplug them, which can be annoying. You can find ceramic sockets at hardware stores, and they are becoming more common in pet stores, especially ones that specialize in herps.

Another drawback to these devices is the price. They are expensive, although they are durable and last a long time. At the time of this writing, I have one that has been heating my tortoises for almost ten years.

Lighting

You may be puzzled that there is a lighting section when heat lamps were already covered in this chapter. This section is not about lights used for heating but about lights that provide your bearded dragon with critical ultraviolet light.

Ultraviolet Light: Why Is It Important?

Ultraviolet light (UV) is a type of light that is beyond the range of human sight. The sun produces UV, and this is the part of sunlight that causes sunburn. Different wavelengths of UV are given different designations by letter. The two types that reptile keepers are most concerned with are the A waves (UVA) and the B waves (UVB).

When a reptile basks, he is absorbing more than just heat from the sun. He's

Don't Be Fooled by Full Spectrum

Lightbulbs that are labeled "full spectrum" are not the same as those that produce UVA and UVB. "Full spectrum" simply means that the light appears close to natural sunlight. It doesn't mean that the bulb produces any UV light whatsoever. Also, bulbs manufactured for growing plants indoors do not produce UVB. Stick with bulbs that are manufactured for use with reptiles and are guaranteed to produce UVB.

also absorbing the UV light. While UV can be harmful, it is also beneficial. The UVA rays seem to be psychologically beneficial, being responsible for normal behavior patterns. They play a role in regulating breeding and basking. Additionally, it is believed that some reptiles can see this type of light and may need it to recognize the normal appearance of food, mates, territorial markers, etc. The UVB rays are physically beneficial. They enable lizards (and humans, birds, and many other animals) to make vitamin D. Without vitamin D, a lizard cannot absorb calcium from his food and will become calcium deficient and develop metabolic bone disease. (See Chapter 5.)

Providing UV

When housed indoors, bearded dragons cannot bask in natural sunlight. They need some other source of UV or their health will suffer. While you may think that you can just put your beardie in the window on sunny afternoons, this will not work. Most types of glass block the transmission of UV waves. The only way to provide your pet with necessary UV is to use a lightbulb that generates UVA and UVB. There are two types: fluorescent bulbs and mercury vapor bulbs.

Fluorescent Bulbs

Specially made fluorescent bulbs can be used to provide beardies with needed UV. These tube-shaped bulbs are available at most pet stores and can also be found at herp shows and online vendors. You will also have to buy a fluorescent light fixture to house the bulb. Pet stores carry these fixtures, as do hardware stores.

When buying the bulb, it's best to choose one made specifically for use with reptiles (although the ones made for birds might work in a pinch). Make sure that it produces UVB; many produce only UVA. Most often the bulbs express the amount of UVB as a percentage. Look for one that produces 5 to 10 percent UVB. The bulb that you use should be half to three-quarters the length of the enclosure. In a really large enclosure, plan to use multiple bulbs. Using multiple bulbs is not a bad idea anyway, as it ensures that your dragon is getting enough UVB; also, bearded dragons like a brightly lit enclosure.

When you are setting up the fluorescent bulb, there are a few things to keep in mind. The farther away from the bulb, the more the UV light degrades. These bulbs are most effective when they are about 1 foot (30.5 cm) from your dragon (unless the manufacturer states otherwise). In a tall cage, you may need to angle a climbing branch up near the light or build some kind of platform

In nature, bearded dragons often bask on tree limbs. You can angle a climbing branch under your beardie's lights so that he can engage in this activity within his cage.

that he can climb up on so that he can get near enough to the light.

In nature, the sun provides both heat and UV, so a bearded dragon is adapted to a situation in which he gets his light and heat at the same time. To mimic this in his enclosure, put the UV light such that it is near the basking site.

Fluorescent bulbs don't produce UVB forever. They will keep emitting light long after they have stopped putting out UVB. You should replace your fluorescent bulb after about six months. After six months, the amount of UVB the bulb emits will have declined to such a level as to be almost worthless.

Mercury Vapor Bulbs

Mercury vapor bulbs are a type of incandescent light that screws into a light socket and generates heat, visible light, and high amounts of UVA and UVB. The ones manufactured for use with reptiles are usually named so that the word "sun" or both "heat" and "UV" are in the name.

One of the best features of these bulbs is that, because they produce both heat and light, you may need only one bulb for your enclosure. (This will depend on the size of the enclosure, of course.) Because of the heat and high levels of UV generated, these bulbs should not be any closer than 18 inches (45.7 cm) to your lizard. Also, you must be sure that your dragon can get completely out of the light when he so desires. As much as possible, avoid looking directly into the light.

Night Lights

There are lightbulbs manufactured for use as nighttime heaters on herp cages. They are most often red or blue bulbs. The light they generate supposedly does not interfere with a reptile's day/night cycle. Some recent research suggests that this might be false. Because of this and because most of the time bearded dragons do not need additional heat at night, I don't recommend using these bulbs. However, they are excellent for viewing nocturnal herps, such as red-eyed tree frogs and crested geckos.

Mercury vapor bulbs are more expensive than fluorescents. However, they can last a lot longer. Replace them according to the manufacturer's instructions—normally these bulbs need replacement after one or two years. Mercury vapor bulbs are fragile, so be careful whenever you are moving the bulb about, especially if it is still hot. You cannot install a dimmer switch on one of these bulbs to control the output of light or heat.

Much like a ceramic heat emitter, the heat generated by mercury vapor bulbs can melt a plastic socket. To avoid risking a fire, use only a ceramic light socket with these bulbs.

Photoperiod

Like humans, most animals are healthiest when exposed to a regular cycle of light and dark; bearded dragons are no exception. Creatures of tropical and subtropical deserts, they thrive in conditions with long, hot days. The amount of light they receive during a 24-hour day is the photoperiod. To create a photoperiod, you will need to turn the lights on in the morning and off at night, and you should do so on a regular schedule. This will be easiest if you set the lights and any other heating devices on a timer.

Bearded dragons do best when they have a photoperiod of 12 to 14 hours of light each day and 10 to 12 hours of darkness. To reflect conditions in nature, you can shorten the daylight

hours in the winter to as little as 10 hours. While this is not normally necessary, this is a good idea if you are planning to breed your dragons. A darker, cooler winter followed by a brighter, hotter spring will usually stimulate them to breed.

Humidity

As you might guess, bearded dragons are adapted to living in fairly dry conditions. They do not do well when kept in humid enclosures, usually developing skin and/or respiratory infections. So for the most part you will be keeping your beardie's cage as dry as possible. The best way to do this is to make sure that the cage is well ventilated. If you are using a glass aquarium, a screen top is ideal; don't use a glass or plastic lid. If you are using some other type of housing, make sure that there is adequate

Turn off your beardie's lights at night so that he can sleep. The cage should be dark for 10 to 12 hours each day.

Disinfection 101

If you find the perfect rock or branch for your beardie's tank lying around your yard, you first have to eliminate any potentially harmful organisms that might be living on it or in it. These can include parasites, such as mites and ticks, and pathogenic microorganisms, such as bacteria and fungi. If you don't disinfect the item, there is a chance your lizard could become ill. Some experts recommend disinfecting even items you buy from pet stores because you don't know what they've come in contact with while they were in the store.

Before you disinfect the item, you need to give it a good cleaning. This is important to remove dirt, fungi, and other undesirable materials. If you are going to disinfect with bleach, dirt and organic matter can prevent the bleach from fully disinfecting the item. Wash the item thoroughly in hot water. Clean out all the nooks and crannies—an old toothbrush does a great job with this. You can use a mild soap when cleaning rocks, but you should use plain water on branches and other pieces of wood. Allow the item to air-dry completely.

Now you can disinfect it. There are two main ways of doing this: with bleach or with heat. The method you use is up to you, but one may be more appropriate for some items than others.

If you are going to bleach the item, make a solution of 10 percent bleach (1 part bleach to 9 parts water). Immerse the item completely in this solution. (Use gloves to avoid irritating your hands.) Alternatively, you can put the bleach solution in a misting bottle and thoroughly mist the item with the solution. Label the misting bottle so that it never gets used for another purpose. The second method works well with large items that would be difficult to completely submerge. Allow the bleach to soak on the item for at least 15 minutes—more time won't hurt and may be even better. Afterward, rinse the item at least three or four times in water. You want to rinse it until you can no longer smell any bleach on the item. Allow it to air-dry, preferably in the sunlight. Afterward, it's ready to serve as a cage furnishing.

To use heat to disinfect the item, wrap the clean and dry item in aluminum foil. Place it in the oven set to 250°F (121°C). Bake the item for 30 to 60 minutes. Shut the oven off and allow the item to cool down to room temperature. When it is cooled off, you can take off the foil; do so carefully because the item may be hot under the foil. If so, let it sit until it is completely cool. Once it is cooled and unwrapped, it is safe to add to your beardie's enclosure. While baking, some items will begin to smell pretty bad, which is one of the drawbacks of this method.

Both of these methods work very well at getting rid of parasites and pathogens. While there is still a tiny chance that some pathogens survived the treatment, disinfecting items with one of these methods is the best way to keep infectious disease away from your dragon.

ventilation. Additionally, use a small water bowl.

Of course, even in the desert it rains occasionally. There is no harm in misting your bearded dragon once in a while to simulate a rainy day. This can help him shed, so you can mist the cage lightly when he's actively shedding. He'll likely appreciate the change in his weather. Similarly, if he knocks over his water bowl there is no need to panic, thinking that the temporary boost in humidity is going to make him ill. As long as you keep the cage dry most of the time, a few hours in this dragon-made sauna will be okay.

Cage Furnishings

A bearded dragon in an enclosure that is properly warmed and lit and given a nutritious diet will survive, but he won't be very happy. Nor will your enclosure look at all interesting. Hide boxes, branches, rocks, plants, and other cage furnishings will turn your cage into a dragon's den.

Hide Boxes

Bearded dragons are fearless and outgoing creatures, but they occasionally want to retire from the public eye. A hide box provides your lizard with a space where he can do just that. This may not literally be a box—although it can be—but it is a semi-enclosed place in which he can go to feel safe and secure. Any hide box you use

must be big enough to enter and exit easily. It also shouldn't allow in much light; the idea is to create a dark, cozy place for your beardie.

An endless variety of suitable hide boxes are available. Your local pet store should have a good selection, and an even wider range can be found at herp expos and via online retailers. Some hide boxes are more or less literally boxes. They are made from plastic and have an opening that your beardie and crawl in and out of. Some are colored and textured to resemble desert stones, while others (usually less expensive) are more utilitarian.

Other materials besides products specifically designed as hide boxes can serve as such. You can use large

Although bearded dragons are outgoing lizards, they still enjoy having shelters and hiding places in their enclosures.

tubes of cork bark. This durable, lightweight bark is a renewable resource—the trees are not killed to harvest the bark. However, large pieces can be expensive, and cork bark is a bit hard to clean.

Pet stores often sell hollowed-out log halves that can serve as beardie hiding places as well, although finding cork bark tubes or log halves big enough for an adult dragon may be a bit of a challenge. A herp expo may be your best bet.

Some keepers use large-diameter PVC pipes for hide boxes. While not the most attractive items, they are durable and relatively inexpensive. You can find them at hardware and home improvement stores. You can easily cut PVC piping to fit the space you have in your enclosure. By pushing one end beneath the substrate (assuming that you are using sand or something similar), you can create a ready-made burrow for your dragon. If you want the piping to blend in with your cage decor, you can paint it with nontoxic paint.

Almost anything can serve as a beardie's hide box, as long as it is made of nontoxic material, has no sharp edges, and is the right size for your dragon. You could make your own out of lumber. I've seen hide boxes made from large plastic storage containers. You could make some interesting caves out of pottery, if that's one of your skills. One of my hide boxes is a large section of clay drainage pipe that I found in a ditch (and cleaned and disinfected before I put it to use).

Climbing Branches

Bearded dragons like to climb, so you should include a climbing branch or two in your beardie's enclosure. One branch should be angled up toward the light so that he can bask on his branches as he would do in the outback. Ideally, your climbing branches will be larger in diameter than the width of your dragon. This will give him enough space to rest comfortably on the branch. In a large cage, you can have multiple branches of varying sizes, as long as the main branch under the basking light is the right diameter for your dragon.

You can use the driftwood pieces sold at pet stores, find some interesting pieces of wood at herp expos, or collect your own from your yard or local woodlands. No matter where you get your branches, clean and sanitize them before putting them into your dragon's lair. (See sidebar "Disinfection 101" on ways to disinfect the items in your beardie's cage.) Another thing to consider is that some types of wood may be toxic, so know what you are collecting. Avoid using any conifers— pines, cedars, junipers, hemlocks, yews, etc.—red maple, black locust, laurels, chinaberry, and oleander. Obviously, anything that has thorns or spines is unsafe (unless you remove them). Some types of wood known to be safe include grape vines, oak, willow, lilac, apple, and maple.

As an alternative to branches, some keepers use shelves as climbing and basking platforms for their beardies. These usually have ramps or branches leading up to them. The shelves are normally made of wood, but some keepers have used plastic or Plexiglas shelves successfully. The shelves are usually attached to the walls of the enclosure with screws or nails (obviously not possible in a glass aquarium). To use shelves in a glass aquarium, you could hang them from the side with metal wire or something similar. Be sure that any ramp leading up to the shelf has a rough surface so that your beardie can climb it with ease.

Rocks

The desert and scrubby habitats of bearded dragons abound with rocks of all shapes and sizes. A nice rock or two can create an interesting and natural appearance in your dragon's cage. Aside from the aesthetic benefits of having rocks in your bearded dragon's enclosure, they provide him with a more complex and stimulating habitat. Also, climbing over some rocks will help wear down his toenails, making it less likely you'll have to trim them.

Almost any rocks can be used, but the ones available from pet stores are safe and have a nice desert look to them. As with branches, any rocks collected from the outdoors will need to be cleaned and sterilized before placing them in the cage.

If you are using rocks in your beardie's enclosure, there are some safety issues to be aware of. First, use only rocks that are too large to be swallowed. Select nice large ones that your dragon can climb over, hide

Rocks give an enclosure a natural look; they also provide climbing surfaces and help wear down your dragon's claws.

behind, and bask upon. Go over every rock carefully, looking for any sharp points that could injure your lizard— use your fingers to feel for these hazards. In many cases, you can use a metal file to smooth out rough or pointed edges. If the rock has any flaky or crumbling areas where little bits are falling off or look like they could, do not use that rock. Those little rock bits are a definite impaction hazard. Porous types of stone are fine to use, but they will be difficult to clean. Also, if the pores or crannies are large enough, crickets and other feeder insects can hide in them.

Bearded Dragons

Another safety issue rocks pose is injury to your dragon. If you stack rocks to make a cave or some type of visually interesting formation, you have to ensure that they cannot shift or fall. A large rock falling on him could cause a serious injury or death. Also, be aware that he might decide to try to burrow underneath the rock. If the rock then settles down on top of him, he could be crushed or suffocate. All rocks should rest on the bottom of the cage—not on top of the substrate—so that your beardie cannot tunnel beneath them. If you want a pile or stack of rocks, use a nontoxic epoxy to fix them in place to prevent them from falling onto your pet.

Basking Rock

As discussed in the heating section earlier, it's a good idea to have a flat rock beneath the basking light. This rock will get nice and hot for your dragon to bask on.

Caves

It seems appropriate to have a cave in a dragon enclosure, and a stone cave makes a nice hide box. Some companies make stone (or stone-like resin) caves, but you could also make your own. Select rocks that are the same type and similar in color for the most natural-looking effect. Use a nontoxic epoxy to fix them together into the size and shape you desire, leaving one side open as an entrance. You should probably not include a bottom on the cave, because doing so will make the cave difficult to clean. When the rocks are all in place and the epoxy completely dry, smooth out the surface to a natural appearance with coarse sandpaper. When there is no longer any odor from the epoxy, it is safe to put the cave into the enclosure.

Bricks and Similar Items

If you are not trying to make a naturalistic enclosure, you can use bricks, patio blocks, or cinder blocks as substitute rock structures. Using some epoxy, you can create a nice

Beardies climb frequently in nature, and yours will appreciate a climbing branch or two in his enclosure.

cave or other structure with bricks. Cinder blocks have hollow areas that your dragon can hide in while he uses the surface for climbing and basking. Because all of these items are so heavy, be very careful if using them inside a glass aquarium.

Plants

Many keepers wish to create naturalistic enclosures with sand substrates, weathered rocks, and live desert plants to turn their beardie's enclosure into a beautiful showpiece in their living rooms. Unfortunately, this does not usually work with bearded dragons. You consider the plants to be beautiful decorations; your bearded dragon considers them tasty salad. Any plant you put into his enclosure will be sampled, and if he likes it, eaten. If it does not agree with his palate, he'll use it as climbing material, and unless the plant is very large and sturdy, it will be shredded by his claws and trampled under his weight. Lastly, a beardie's digging activity will often uproot live plants. In an indoor enclosure, it's nearly impossible to keep live plants with beardies.

You may be able to use artificial plants. Sometimes bearded dragons will nibble on them, so watch when you first put an artificial plant into the enclosure. If your dragon just licks it and moves on, that's fine. If he nibbles it, you should probably use something else or he could become impacted from swallowing bits of the plant. Realistic-looking plastic and silk plants are available at pet stores and herp expos.

Food and Water Bowls

You will need a few bowls for giving your dragon his vegetables and water. For the vegetables, you can use a bowl or something like a paper plate or flat piece of cardboard. I prefer the bowl because it's less likely that the veggies will get dragged through the substrate and that your dragon will walk over them (just less likely; both eventualities will still sometimes occur). You will also

FAMILY-FRIENDLY TIP

But I Want Him in My Room

When you bring your new dragon home, it is likely that your children will want to set up his cage in one of their rooms. Unless the child is an older teen, this is not the best idea. If the dragon is in a kid's room, it will be more difficult for a responsible adult to oversee his care. By putting the enclosure in a more central location, you can make sure that the lizard is being fed and watered daily and that the temperatures are in the correct range. Additionally, you can be sure that the bearded dragon is neither being handled too much nor being ignored.

need a bowl for his water.

What type of bowls should you use? There are a few options. The heavy-duty ceramic bowls sold in pet stores—usually in the small animal section but sometimes with the herp supplies—are great choices. They are really easy to clean and durable. In fact, they will last for years, provided you don't drop them on a hard surface. Stainless steel bowls are good, but dragons can often flip them over. Plastic bowls are not the best choice. They eventually get scratched, and the scratches harbor bacteria. Additionally, it can be difficult to get dried pieces of fruit and vegetables off them, and bearded dragons can usually flip over a plastic bowl.

The food bowl must be large enough to hold a day's worth of salad for your dragon. Of course, this means that adult dragons require larger bowls than young dragons. The water bowl should be only as big as it needs to be to provide enough water for the day. A large water bowl can raise the humidity in the cage too much.

It is convenient to have an extra set of bowls on hand. It makes giving your pet fresh food and water every day a bit easier. You can fill the clean bowls with food and water, put them in the cage, and pop the old ones out and into the sink or dishwasher for later cleaning.

In a large enclosure, you can use cinder or patio blocks as cage furnishings.

Cleaning and Maintenance

One of the most important aspects of bearded dragon care is regularly cleaning the enclosure. If feces and bits of uneaten food build up in the enclosure, bacteria and fungi will

Clean and refill your dragon's food and water bowls daily and whenever they become soiled.

proliferate, and eventually your beardie will get sick. Also, if your beardie is forced to walk through his own wastes, you'll be exposed to those wastes every time you pick him up. For the sake of his health and yours, keep the cage as clean as possible.

How often you clean the cage will depend on a number of factors. One of the major ones is the substrate you use. Substrates like sand and recycled paper bedding can be spot cleaned daily and will need complete replacement only every month or so. Newspaper and similar products will likely need daily replacement.

It's handy to have a small cage or carrier on hand. You can put your beardie in it while you perform cleaning duties, which will keep him safe and contained while you work in his enclosure. You probably won't need to take him out while you spot clean or change out the food and water bowls, but some beardies are too curious and will constantly be in the way. If that's the case, you'll need to put him into the carrier before beginning any type of enclosure maintenance.

Daily Tasks

Each day, give the cage a quick inspection. If you see any feces or bits of uneaten food, remove them. Feces in the substrate can be scooped out with a spatula or spoon; the feces-lifting item should be designated for this task only! If using a newspaper substrate, remove wet and soiled pieces and replace with clean ones. Feces on climbing branches or rocks can be wiped off with a paper towel. Check that the temperatures are in the proper range, and verify that all heating and lighting devices are working correctly. Clean the food and water bowls, refill with fresh food and water, and return them to the cage.

Weekly Tasks

If using a cage liner as your substrate, remove it for cleaning. Wipe any wet areas of the cage bottom with a paper towel and put in a clean cage liner. Use a damp paper towel to wipe the sides of the cage—inside and outside—so that the view into the enclosure isn't impaired by dirt, dust, or smudges.

Monthly Tasks

Do a thorough cleaning and disinfecting once a month. Take out all of the cage furnishings. You can clean and disinfect these items in the bathtub or outdoors, depending on your home situation and preference. Each item should be soaked and scrubbed in plain hot water. Make sure that you remove all bits of dirt, feces, and what have you. Rinse them well. To disinfect them, you can either submerge them in a tub of bleach and water or mist them with a 10-percent bleach and water solution. In either case, make sure that the bleach solution gets all over the furnishings, into every crevice and cranny. Allow the bleach to sit on the items for 15 to 30 minutes. Afterward, rinse thoroughly until no bleach smell remains. Let the furnishings air-dry.

You also need to disinfect the enclosure at this time. Remove all of the substrate. If you use sand or recycled paper bedding, dispose of it appropriately; use a vacuum cleaner to suck up any remaining dust these two substrates leave behind. Wash the enclosure in hot water to remove all dirt and wastes. Soak the cage in a bleach solution, and rinse as you would for the furnishings. Dry it off as much as you can and then allow it to air-dry the rest of the way. To help the cage dry faster, turn the heat lamps on. Once it is dry, replace the substrate and put the furnishings back inside. Last, put your dragon back in—he'll probably be very happy to be back in his lair.

This is a good time to dust off the light fixtures, sweep behind the cage, clean the walls around the cage, etc. Be sure to dust off any power strips you are using too. Change the bulbs now if necessary. If the cage is on a stand, move it out and sweep underneath it.

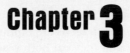

Chapter 3

A Dragon's

Diet

Most keepers find the feeding of their bearded dragons to be one of the most fun aspects of their care. Bearded dragons eat with a comical gusto. However, providing one of these lizards with a healthy diet is more complex than just tossing in some crickets every day. Like humans, bearded dragons need a wide range of different foodstuffs to remain healthy.

What Dragons Eat

Bearded dragons are omnivores, meaning they eat both plants and animals. In nature, they consume the leaves, shoots, and flowers of native plant life. Bearded dragons also eat fruits when they can find them. Additionally, they will eat any small animals they can catch and kill. The majority of the animals they eat are insects and other arthropods (spiders, scorpions, centipedes, etc.), but they are known to prey upon small mammals, nestling birds, frogs, lizards, snakes, worms, and possibly snails as well. If a beardie can catch it, he'll eat it.

The diet you feed your bearded dragon should be similar in many ways to his natural diet. Of course, it is unlikely that you will be able to supply native Australian shrubs or grasshoppers, but you can provide a wide diversity of plant and animal materials that will give your beardie all the nutrients he needs for a long and healthy life. Let's break down the diet into its various components and then discuss how to put them together to form a superb dragon menu.

Fruits and Vegetables

A substantial portion of your beardie's diet should be composed of fruits and vegetables—mostly vegetables. With just a few exceptions, everything in your local grocer's produce department can be used as dragon food. Some choices are better than others, and there are a few types that you shouldn't feed your dragon at all. Other types can be used as everyday staples on your

Bearded dragons require a varied diet that includes both animal and plant matter.

pet's menu. The reasons that a particular fruit or vegetable falls into one category or another vary but for the most part are related to the nutritional content—with calcium being perhaps the nutrient that deserves the most attention—and the oxalate content, or toxicity.

All fruits and vegetables you feed your bearded dragon should be washed, peeled if necessary, and cut into appropriately sized pieces. Some hard vegetables, such as squashes and carrots, will need to be grated before serving. Feeding your dragon organic produce is strongly encouraged. There are now several good studies showing that organic produce is both safer and more nutritious than produce treated with synthetic pesticides and fertilizers.

Feed your dragon fresh produce as much as possible. Frozen is okay, but freezing does destroy some of the nutrients—thiamin in particular. Avoid canned vegetables because these usually contain too much salt.

The Importance of Calcium

You are probably aware that calcium is a mineral that is essential to our health and well-being. It is just as important to your bearded dragon's health too. As in humans and other vertebrates, in bearded dragons calcium makes up the bulk of the skeleton, plays a role in the transmission of nerve impulses, is necessary for muscle contraction, and has other functions. If your beardie isn't getting enough calcium, his health will deteriorate.

Unfortunately, it isn't just the amount of calcium that's important. It's the ratio of calcium to phosphorus. Ideally, the ratio of calcium to phosphorus in a bearded dragon's diet should be between 1.5:1 and 2:1. Don't be alarmed by those numbers—you won't need to know the chemical composition of your dragon's food to feed him correctly. In general, you just want to be sure that you are feeding him a diet high in calcium and lower in phosphorus. Food items that are particularly high or low in these minerals are noted as such in this chapter.

The Expert Knows

Eat Your Vegetables

If you obtain your bearded dragon from someone who was not well informed on his care, he may have been fed only crickets and maybe other insects. Dragons like this sometimes do not recognize vegetables as food. Eating only insects is not healthy for a bearded dragon in the long term. To coax him to try vegetables, there are a couple of tricks you can try. One is to add insects to the food bowl with the vegetables. This works best with mealworms or other insects that cannot easily get out of the bowl. When your beardie eats the insects, he'll get some pieces of vegetable in his mouth. After a few times, he'll realize that the vegetables are food. You can also try wiggling some veggies to stimulate his interest. (Keep your fingers out of the way.) If those two suggestions don't work, try making your dragon really hungry. Don't feed him for two or three days—but do this only if your dragon is totally healthy and in good weight. After two or three days, put a bowlful of veggies in his cage. He should come around and eat them.

A Dragon's Diet

Leafy green vegetables are some of the best items you can feed your dragon.

The Issue of Oxalates

Many plants contain chemicals called oxalates or oxalic acids. Oxalates are of special concern for bearded dragon owners because these chemicals make calcium unavailable for digestion. So even though there is calcium present in the food the lizard eats, it passes right through the gut without being absorbed. Therefore, feeding a bearded dragon plants that have a high oxalate content can result in his suffering from a calcium deficiency even if there is plenty of calcium in the diet.

It is impossible to avoid feeding your dragon any oxalates, but you can limit the amount in his diet by not feeding plants known to contain high concentrations of these chemicals. The following fruits and vegetables have very high levels of oxalates: beet and beet greens, chard, kiwis, parsley, spinach, and star fruits (carambola). While you can feed your dragon high-oxalate plants on rare occasions or in tiny quantities, it is best to avoid them altogether. If you do give your beardie a bit of spinach or a piece of kiwi, add extra calcium supplements to his food that day (more on supplements later in this chapter).

Goitrogens

Some vegetables are goitrogens, meaning that they interfere with the body's ability to absorb iodine, resulting in impaired function of the thyroid gland. Many vegetables are somewhat goitrogenic, but vegetables in the genus *Brassica* seem to be especially problematic. These include bok choy (Chinese cabbage), broccoli, brussels sprouts, cabbage, cauliflower, kale, kohlrabi, radishes, and rapini (broccoli rabe). To prevent the risk of causing an iodine deficiency, these vegetables should not be fed to bearded dragons frequently. Feeding them occasionally is fine because these plants are highly nutritious. Interestingly, mustard greens and collard greens are also in the genus *Brassica*, but they do not seem to cause problems for lizards.

Leafy Green Vegetables

The bulk of the plant matter you feed your beardie should be leafy green vegetables (e.g., collard greens, dandelion greens, endive). A large percentage of the diet of wild bearded dragons consists of leaves and shoots, and feeding your pet plenty of leafy greens simulates this natural diet.

Which greens are best for beardies? Choose the ones that have the most calcium and the lowest phosphorus and oxalates. The following are among the best greens to feed to bearded dragons, and you can feed them daily: dandelion greens, collard greens, mustard greens, turnip greens, endive, escarole, and arugula (rocket). Other good choices in this category include chicory, cilantro, borage, and radicchio. Some greens that can be fed occasionally are bok choy, cabbage (all types), celery leaves (not the stalk), grape leaves, kale, leeks, and watercress.

Although lettuces—including iceberg, green leaf, romaine, and others—are leafy greens, they are poor choices for feeding bearded dragons.

Lettuces are low in many nutrients, essentially being little more than water and fiber. Feed more nutritious greens instead.

Other Vegetables

The majority of the plant matter you feed your beardie should be in the form of leafy greens, but many other vegetables make great additions to his diet. As with the greens, some choices are better than others. Among the very best vegetables for beardies are winter squashes. These include acorn, butternut, delicata, hubbard, kabocha, and spaghetti squashes—there are many other types. Although we tend to think of it as a separate food, pumpkin is a winter squash too. Pumpkin is slightly less nutritious than the other squashes but still is a wonderful food for your dragon. These squashes are high in vitamins A, C, and several of

Dandelion leaves and flowers have loads of calcium and vitamin A, making them a great dragon food.

Spice It Up

Although we don't usually think of herbs as leafy greens, they are just the leaves of plants. Many herbs make fine additions to your dragon's diet, but they should not, as a general rule, be fed as a staple. Instead, feed them occasionally. Bearded dragons seem to enjoy these pungent treats. Some safe herbs you can offer your lizard include:

- **basil**
- **dill**
- **mints (such as spearmint and peppermint)**
- **oregano**
- **tarragon**
- **thyme**

the B vitamins, as well as being excellent sources of fiber, potassium, and iron. Because squashes are so hard, you should grate them before feeding to your dragon.

A vegetable you may never have seen but is well worth seeking out for your dragon is cactus pads. These are the leaves of the prickly pear cactus and are used in the cuisines of many Latin American countries. If your local grocer doesn't carry

them, try a Hispanic grocery store. Prickly pear cactus grows wild in the western United States and in arid areas of Central and South America, so harvesting or growing your own may be an option if you live in one of those regions. Cactus pads are loaded with calcium and fiber and can be fed daily. Use a sharp knife to remove the spines (carefully!) and chop the pad into bite-sized chunks. The spines are easier to remove when the pads are lightly steamed first.

Most other vegetables are fine to feed your beardie. Some good choices include asparagus, bell peppers, carrots (grated), okra, sweet potato (lightly steamed), yams (lightly steamed), and zucchini. Except on rare occasions, it is best to avoid feeding corn (high in phosphorus), cucumbers (low in most nutrients), and potatoes (high in phosphorus).

Fruits

We humans normally think of fruits as a healthy snack, and they are when compared to potato chips and candy bars. However, fruits are largely composed of sugar and water. Some fruits do have a good supply of vitamins and/or minerals, but they are still loaded with sugar. For this reason, it is best to think of fruits as a treat for your bearded dragon rather than as a main part of a meal.

The best fruits to feed him are those that are high in vitamins and minerals—especially calcium—and that have the lowest levels of oxalates and other troublesome substances. Among

Please Do Eat the Flowers

Wild bearded dragons eat various types of flowers when they are in season. A number of familiar flowers make good food for bearded dragons. These include:

- carnations
- chamomile
- chicory
- clover
- dahlias
- dandelions
- day lilies (not the similar-looking tiger lily)
- geraniums
- gladiolas
- hibiscus
- hollyhocks
- impatiens
- lavender
- marigolds
- nasturtiums
- pansies
- petunias
- roses
- roses of Sharon
- violets (not African violets)

Although all of the listed flowers are safe to feed to beardies, they should be used as treats rather than as staple items in the diet. The reason for this is that there is insufficient research on the nutritional contents of flowers to know how beneficial they are for bearded dragons. There are a few exceptions. Dandelions, hibiscus (including the leaves), and nasturtiums are all high in calcium and other nutrients and seem to be low in oxalates, so they can be fed fairly often.

Never feed your dragon flowers that come from a florist shop. These flowers are often treated with preservatives that could be toxic to your lizard. Also, be careful when harvesting your own flowers. You must make sure that the area from which you collect flowers has not been sprayed with any pesticides, herbicides, or fertilizers because these items can be harmful to beardies. Harvesting flowers from the side of the road is also not a good idea. They are likely contaminated with fuel, oil, and other chemicals from traffic. The best way to provide your dragon with edible flowers is to grow them yourself.

the best are blackberries, figs, papayas, and prickly pears (cactus fruit). These four are nutrient powerhouses and have high levels of calcium. Most other fruits are perfectly fine when served as the occasional treat.

Bananas, grapes, pomegranates, raspberries, and tomatoes are best fed sparingly because they are low in calcium or high in oxalates or phosphorus. Oranges and grapefruits are highly nutritious and calcium rich; however, they often upset the digestion of bearded dragons, resulting in runny and smelly stools. If you want to feed your dragon these nutritious fruits, offer very small pieces at first to see how his digestive system reacts. As mentioned earlier, kiwis and star fruits are extremely high in oxalates, so you should probably skip feeding them altogether.

When feeding fruits to your dragon, always remove the pit or seeds. They are choking and impaction hazards. Also, some fruits—apples, cherries, peaches, and others—have toxic seeds or pits.

Toxic Fruits and Vegetables

Most of the items in your local produce department are safe to feed your bearded dragon. Some may be better than others, but very few will actually harm your beloved pet. If you accidentally grab parsley instead of cilantro, you can get away with feeding it to him for a day or two until you can get back to the store.

However, there are a few fruits and vegetables that are not safe to feed—or are at least suspected of being toxic. Never feed these veggies to your dragon: avocados, chives, eggplant (raw), garlic, mushrooms, onions (including scallions), and rhubarb. Rhubarb is deadly for beardies, and avocados kill birds, so why take a chance? The others are suspected of being somewhat toxic to beardies, so avoid feeding them. Additionally, the leaves, stems, and foliage of eggplant, potatoes, and tomatoes are somewhat toxic—they are in the same family as deadly nightshade!

Animal Foods

In nature, bearded dragons eat a wide array of other animals along with their leaves and flowers. You will have to

Feed your dragon various fruits as treats, rather than as staple items in the diet.

You must be careful to offer young dragons appropriately sized prey. The cricket in this photo looks too large for this baby beardie.

supply some prey animals to your pet beardie to ensure that he is getting proper nutrition. This does not mean feeding him some hamburger meat (although a beardie might eat that). It instead means providing insects or other small animals. In most cases, you will be offering these items while they are still alive. The movement of the prey stimulates beardies' hunting instincts, and they seem quite excited when chasing crickets around their cage.

There are quite a number of different prey species available for feeding bearded dragons. As with fruits and vegetables, strive to vary the types of prey you offer. Unfortunately, most pet stores offer only crickets, mealworms, and mice, which are not an optimal choice. To provide other types of live food to your dragon, you will likely need to turn to the Internet. You should be able to find more than a few live insect suppliers who will ship to your door. Another good source of feeder insects is your local herpetological society. It is highly likely that a few members of the society cultivate their own live foods and would be happy to share (or sell) some of the feeders they produce with other herp keepers.

Prey Size

It is very important that the feeders you give your beardie are of the appropriate size. A good rule of thumb is to offer prey that is no larger in any dimension than the width of your dragon's head. This is especially true of hatchling and very young dragons. Feeding baby dragons prey that is too large can cause injuries and

Bad Bugs

If you decide to feed your bearded dragon insects and other arthropods you catch yourself, you must familiarize yourself with those types that can injure, sicken, or even kill your pet. As a general rule, do not feed brightly colored insects—they are likely to be poisonous—or any species that stings. Another tip is not to give your dragon an insect that is feeding on a poisonous plant—that insect is likely poisonous as well. If you are in doubt about the safety of any potential food item you catch, it is safer not to feed that item. The list below contains a few common types of insects and other arthropods that you must avoid feeding because they are known to be harmful. This is not a complete list, only a list of those you are most likely to encounter.

- bees
- centipedes
- fireflies (lightning bugs)
- ladybird beetles (ladybugs)
- monarch butterflies
- spiky or fuzzy caterpillars
- wasps

even death. Adult beardies are large enough that very few insects will be too big for them to eat.

On the flip side, prey that is too small may not interest your dragon. If an insect is really tiny, it may not be worth it to your lizard to expend the energy chasing it.

Gut Loading

When you come home from the pet store with a bag of juicy crickets in hand, you just need to open the bag and dump them into your beardie's cage, right? Wrong! Crickets and other feeder insects fresh from the store (or the shipping container) usually have not been fed a nutritious diet for some time. They are essentially little more than bags of protein, fat, and water, lacking in most vitamins and minerals.

You will need to remedy this situation by feeding the insects a highly nutritious diet; this is called gut loading. For gut loading to be effective, the feeder insects need to eat this nutritious diet for at least 24 hours prior to being fed to your beardie. Yes, this means that you will need to set up some type of enclosure for the insects to live in— clearly, keeping a pet bearded dragon is not for the squeamish.

Crickets, roaches, and mealworms are easy to gut load. Other feeder insects such as wax worms and stick insects may be difficult or impossible to gut load. These species and similar ones generally have specialized diets, and if that diet is unavailable, they should just be fed to your lizard quickly after you purchase them. The

Give crickets and other prey insects a nutritious diet before feeding them to your beardie.

details of how to gut load the various types of feeder insects are given in the individual discussions of those insects.

Commercial gut loads for crickets are available at pet stores, and they seem to work fine. Most roaches will eat them too. Many herp keepers prefer to make their own gut loads so that they can tailor the ingredients as desired. Depending on the ingredients you use, it may or may not be cheaper to make your own gut load rather than buying it. If you want to make your own gut load, there are recipes available online.

Crickets

Crickets (*Acheta domestica*) are the most commonly available feeder insect for bearded dragons, and they make a fine staple diet. They are easy to feed and care for while they are being gut loaded. They are not easy to cultivate in the home, however—at least not without significant mess, odor, and

escapees—so it's best to just buy enough for several feedings and set them up in an enclosure for a few days, feeding out the desired number as needed.

Cricket Size

Crickets are available in a range of sizes. Most pet stores carry two or three different sizes, and a wider range is available from cricket farms. Bearded dragons who are at least six months old can normally eat adult crickets with no problem. Up to that age, they will usually require smaller crickets. If you have a hatchling dragon—one who is three months old or younger—you need to be very careful of the cricket size you offer. To get the proper size, you should purchase ones labeled "two weeks old," "fly size," or "quarter-inch." Smaller crickets will be fine, but you will need to feed more of them.

Cricket Care

The size of the enclosure you will need for your crickets will depend on how many you want to keep on hand at once. Most hobbyists keeping only a dragon or two can use a small aquarium—5½ to 10 gallons (21 to 38 l) in size. If you have more dragons, a large plastic storage container works well. Use a screen lid to provide adequate ventilation and to prevent moisture from building up in the container; crickets do not fare well in overly moist environs. A bare-bottom container works best. It's far easier to catch the crickets and to clean the container when there is no substrate present. You will also need some places for the crickets to hide. Crumpled newspaper or empty paper towel and toilet paper rolls work well for this. Room temperatures are fine for crickets as long as they don't drop below 65°F (18.3°C).

Feeding crickets is easy. You can use a commercial gut load or feed a mix of a couple of the following ingredients ground up in a food processor: oatmeal, wheat bran, wheat or rice baby cereal, any whole-grain flour, tropical fish flakes, rodent or rabbit pellets, turtle or tortoise diet, and bee pollen. Add a pinch or two each of powdered calcium and vitamin–mineral supplements. Sprinkle a tablespoonful or so in a corner of the enclosure.

Giving crickets water is more of an issue because they drown easily. There are a number of methods that hobbyists employ, but I'm going to tell you the only one that I've found that works. Provide your crickets with a slice or two of some type of juicy fruit or vegetable on a low plate. The crickets will get plenty of water from the fruit or vegetable and will also acquire more nutrients to pass on to your beardie. Any of the following will serve as a cricket watering station: apples, pears, oranges, melons, broccoli stalks, diced up leafy greens, potatoes, sweet potatoes, and bell peppers. Discard the fruit or vegetable daily and replace with fresh pieces.

In between each batch of crickets you buy, thoroughly clean out the cricket cage. Uneaten food, insect feces, shed bits of exoskeleton, and other detritus will build up in the

This bearded dragon is about to snatch up a king mealworm with his sticky tongue.

cage, and with this material come bacteria. The bacteria will get transferred onto any new crickets put into the cage, and these crickets will transfer bacteria to your dragon. This could cause a gastrointestinal infection or mouth rot. (See Chapter 5.) Part of keeping your beardie healthy is cleaning out the cricket cage—no matter how much you dislike the task.

Mealworms and King Mealworms

Another commonly available feeder insect is the mealworm (*Tenebrio molitor*), which is actually the larva of the darkling beetle and not a worm at all. Mealworms are less than an ideal food for a number of reasons. They have a high chitin content, so they are hard to digest; they are fairly small, which means it takes a lot of them to feed an adult beardie; and they have been implicated in feeding injuries causing paralysis and death in young bearded dragons. Because of the latter, never feed mealworms to bearded dragons who are younger than four months old. On the plus side, mealworms are exceptionally easy to keep and even to culture in a small space.

King mealworms (also called super mealworms, superworms, and giant mealworms) are similar in appearance to mealworms but are much larger— as much as 2 inches (5 cm) long. King mealworms also are the larvae of a beetle, but a different species (*Zophobas morio*). They seem to be more digestible than common mealworms and are just as easy to keep

Little Helping Hands

Feeding bearded dragons is fun, so it's no wonder that children want to participate. There's no reason not to let your kid help with age-appropriate parts of the feeding. For very young children, this means simple tasks such as picking out some fruits and vegetables for the beardie during a shopping trip. An older child could feed out the right number of crickets or superworms and carry the bowls to and from the cage. A responsible teen might be able to completely take over the feeding, although you must still check to be sure that this is getting done when it's supposed to. Feeding a bearded dragon can be fun for the whole family.

61

A Dragon's Diet

and gut load. They are more difficult to raise, though, so few hobbyists bother with trying to raise them.

Mealworm Care

Mealworms and king mealworms are probably the easiest feeder insects to care for. Provide them with a container that is at least 6 inches (15.2 cm) deep. Fill it about half way with some type of flour or grain. You can use any of the following alone or in a mix: oatmeal, any whole-grain flour, wheat bran, and rice or wheat baby cereal. On top of this, place a few slices of apple, potato, or sweet potato to give the worms some moisture. You will need to replace these slices whenever they dry out or become moldy. The container does not need a lid, although most keepers feel more comfortable using one.

At room temperatures, mealworms will eventually pupate and emerge as adult beetles, which can also be fed to your lizard. Left in the container, they will mate and lay eggs, and eventually there will be a fresh supply of mealworms. If you clean out the container every six months or so by sifting out the beetles and worms and replacing the grain substrate, you can keep your mealworm colony going indefinitely. If you refrigerate them, they remain larvae and do not turn into adults. Never refrigerate king mealworms, because doing so will kill this tropical species. King mealworms rarely reproduce without some extra steps that are beyond the scope of this book.

Roaches
Most herp keepers balk at feeding cockroaches to their animals, which is a shame. Roaches are nutritious, have a lower chitin content than many other feeder insects, and compose a large percentage of the natural diet of many reptiles. If you are afraid of having these creepy crawlies infesting your home, relax; we are going to be discussing only a few tropical species that are highly unlikely to infest the average home.

Pet stores normally do not stock roaches, but online herp supply vendors and biological supply companies often sell various cockroaches. A great source for feeder cockroaches is other herp hobbyists; these insects reproduce rapidly, so a fellow keeper may have more roaches than she can use.

Several species of tropical roaches are available in the pet trade. Any species can be fed to bearded dragons as long as it is of the appropriate size. The three that probably make the best food for bearded dragons are the discoid roach, the giant lobster roach, and the orange-spotted roach. These

Many keepers are too squeamish to feed roaches to their dragons, but roaches make excellent feeder insects.

The discoid roach is the species most commonly used for feeding reptiles.

three species all reach a little less than 2 inches (10.2 cm) in length. The discoid roach (*Blaberus discoidalis*) is the most commonly used feeder roach. It is unable to fly or climb up glass, so it is highly unlikely to escape. The giant lobster roach (*Henschoutedenia flexivitta*) can climb glass but is very soft bodied and easy to digest. The orange-spotted roach (*Blaptica dubia*) is sometimes called the speckled roach or the Guyana orange-spotted roach. Like the discoid, it cannot climb glass or fly.

Roach Care

Set up your roaches in an aquarium or plastic storage container. Use a tight-fitting lid that allows plenty of ventilation, such as a screen cover. If the species you are using can climb glass, spread a 1-inch-wide (2.5-cm) layer of petroleum jelly around the rim to prevent them from climbing up to the top. Put a deep layer—2 inches (5 cm) or so—of substrate on the bottom. You can use any one of a number of substrates for cockroaches: potting soil, wood mulch, coconut fiber (coir), recycled paper bedding, or reptile "jungle mix" substrates. Place some paper towel rolls, cardboard egg crates, or similar hiding places on the substrate.

Tropical roaches must be kept between 80° and 90°F (26.7° and 32.2°C). You can use a heat lamp or undertank heater to maintain this temperature. If you use the undertank heater, attach it to the side of the enclosure instead of the bottom. Many roaches dig down into the substrate if they get too warm; if the heater is on the bottom, the roaches will get too hot and die. Mist the roaches daily or every other day to maintain humidity.

Picky Beardies

Most bearded dragons are not selective when it comes to food. They will eat just about anything placed in their bowl and chase down and consume any moving insect. A few beardies are a little pickier—they pick out and eat only certain items from their food bowls. Usually these fussy lizards eat various fruits and brightly colored vegetables but ignore the leafy greens. Much like a child, the beardie can't be allowed to eat just what he wants. If allowed to pick out just certain items over a long period, a beardie could develop nutritional deficiencies. If you have a dragon like this, use a food processor to chop up the veggies into small pieces so that he can't just pick out his favorite ones.

Like crickets, roaches will eat almost anything. Feed them a variety of fruits and vegetables mixed with flake-form fish food, powdered milk, dry dog kibble, tortoise chow, or similar items.

In this type of setup, it is likely the roaches will breed. If you wish to keep your colony going as a source of food for your dragons, it will take several months for there to be a large enough population for you to start harvesting them.

Silkworms

One nutritious feeder insect that is worth seeking out is the silkworm (*Bombyx mori*), the larva of the silk moth. Silkworms are somewhat delicate to handle and tend to be expensive, but they are loaded with calcium. They can reach 3 inches (7.6 cm) in length, so you don't need to feed as many at each meal as you do with other insects. You can obtain silkworms through online insect vendors.

Silkworm Care

Silkworms have a very specialized diet. They eat the leaves of only a few trees, notably the white mulberry. There is a prepared silkworm diet available made primarily of these leaves. Usually silkworms are shipped from the supplier in a container with a supply of food. It is best to just leave them in this container and pick them out to feed your beardies as needed. Keep the container slightly warmer than room temperature, from 75° to 77°F (24° to 25°C). Silkworms grow rapidly, so plan accordingly if you need small ones to feed juvenile dragons.

Other Feeder Insects

Dozens of other feeder insects are available on occasion. As long as the intended meal is the right size for your beardie, it will be fine to feed. Some of the insects you may encounter include wax worms, tomato hornworms, Phoenix worms, houseflies, fruit flies, flour beetles, and stick insects.

Wax Worms

The commonly available wax worm is the larva of the wax moth, a beehive pest. Wax worms are difficult to gut load and high in fat, so feed them to your dragon only as a treat or to fatten up thin or breeding lizards.

Tomato Hornworms

Tomato hornworms (and the very similar tobacco hornworm) are large green caterpillars occasionally available from insect suppliers. They are usually sold in a container with their food. They are big, meaty insects, so you need to feed an adult dragon only two or three of them as a meal. Do not use wild tomato hornworms; they feed on the toxic foliage of tomatoes, potatoes, and tobacco.

Phoenix Worms

Phoenix worms are the larvae of black soldier flies. They are reported to be high in calcium, and more and more pet stores are stocking them. Bearded dragons will eat the worms and the flies they eventually become.

Houseflies

Houseflies—unless you can locate the

flightless variety—escape easily, so you may want to skip using them.

Fruit Flies and Flour Beetles

Flightless fruit flies and flour beetles are very tiny, so their use as bearded dragon food is limited to hatchlings. They make an excellent food for hatchling dragons.

Stick Insects

Stick insects of various species make great food for bearded dragons. However, they tend to be expensive, have specialized diets, and are illegal to keep in some areas. Using native stick insects avoids these issues.

Mice

Many keepers feed mice to their bearded dragon. There is nothing inherently wrong with this practice, but mice are not the best food for bearded dragons. Mice (and other rodents and small mammals for that matter) are high in fat. A dragon fed a lot of mice is likely to become obese and may be more likely to get fatty liver disease. However, feeding the occasional mouse as part of a varied

Tomato hornworms can be very big, so it doesn't take many to make a meal for a beardie.

Catching Dragon Food

Many keepers supplement their beardie's diet by catching insects themselves. This provides some additional variety for your lizard, but there are some potential hazards to avoid. Pet lizards have been sickened and even killed by being fed insects that were caught in areas sprayed with pesticides. Collect your insects from areas that you are absolutely sure are not being sprayed with these chemicals. Catching bugs on your own property is the safest course of action, but insects exposed to pesticides could fly into your yard.

It's smart to become familiar with the poisonous insects that live in your area. Some common toxic insects include monarch butterflies and their caterpillars, ladybugs, and fireflies. Fireflies are especially bad—feeding just one to an adult beardie will kill him! The large, brightly colored lubber grasshoppers are common insects in the southeastern United States and are believed to be toxic.

One other issue is the possibility of introducing parasites to your pet. If you feed wild insects, you should be extra careful in monitoring your dragon's health. If there is a sudden change in his stool—particularly if he gets diarrhea or his stool becomes especially stinky—take him to the vet for a parasite screening. Also, make sure that during your dragon's regular checkup you tell the vet that you are feeding wild-caught insects so she will know to test for parasites.

diet will cause no harm.

If you are going to feed mice to your dragon, you should follow a few simple guidelines.

First, do not feed mice of any size to a young dragon. You can safely start feeding baby mice (called "pinkies" because of their hairless pink skin) to your beardie when he reaches six months of age. Second, make sure that the mouse is the appropriate size—like other prey, mice should be no bigger than the width of your dragon's head. Third, it is highly recommended that you feed only pre-killed mice. Mice in fear of their lives—such as when being attacked by a bearded dragon—will fight back, and their chisel-like teeth are impressive weapons. Although a pinky mouse is defenseless, larger mice can seriously wound or even kill your bearded dragon. Also, feeding pre-killed mice is more humane.

Pet stores that sell reptiles usually sell frozen mice, allowing you to buy a few at a time to have on hand. Thaw the mice by either letting them sit in a warm spot (such as on top of the refrigerator) for a few hours or immersing them in hot—not boiling—water until thawed. The mouse must be thawed all the way through, and it should be room temperature or a little warmer. It may take a bearded dragon a little time to realize that the pre-killed mouse is food. To pique his interest, you can put the mouse in the bowl with his vegetables or try wiggling it a bit. (Use forceps to do this so that your lizard doesn't accidentally nip your finger.)

Lastly, feed mice to your dragon only occasionally. Offer him an appropriately sized mouse no more frequently than once or twice a month.

Commercial Bearded Dragon Diets

Several companies make diets specifically formulated for bearded dragons, and many pet stores carry at least a few brands. There are canned diets and pelleted diets, which are more common. The manufacturers claim that these diets provide complete nutrition for bearded dragons, and you do not need to feed your pet anything else. That may or may not be true, but most of these diets have not been studied over the long term. While using these diets is perfectly acceptable, you should feed them only as part of a varied diet. They are quite convenient for feeding your dragons on really hectic days when you just don't have the time to chop vegetables, for times when you unexpectedly run out of other foods, or for making your pet sitter's life easier when you go on vacation.

Supplements

Feeding a varied diet rich in vegetables and gut-loaded insects is essential to keeping your beardie healthy. However, even such a varied diet is likely not enough to ensure optimal nutrition. To cover any gaps in nutrition, most professional breeders recommend using supplements. It is especially important to supplement the calcium in a bearded dragon's diet. There are a number of types and brands of nutritional supplements available for bearded dragons, and some are better or more necessary than other.

Calcium and Vitamin D3

The most important nutrient to supplement is calcium. Even when feeding a diet full of calcium-rich vegetables, it is likely your lizard is not getting enough of this vital mineral. Purchase a powdered calcium supplement that contains no phosphorus. Most of these supplements also contain vitamin D3. While it is not known for sure whether bearded dragons can absorb vitamin D3 from their diet, it seems to cause no harm. A bearded dragon needs proper lighting so that he can make his own vitamin D3. (See Chapter 2.)

There are other forms of calcium you can give your bearded dragon besides a commercial supplement. One is a cuttlebone. This is the internal shell of the cuttlefish, a squid-like mollusk. You can find it in most pet stores in the bird supply section. To give a cuttlebone to your dragon, either break it into small chunks and then pulverize the chunks in a coffee grinder or scrape it with a knife or file. The dust can be sprinkled over the vegetables or used to coat insects.

(See below.) Another form is antacid tablets. Tums brand is practically pure calcium carbonate—plus some fruit flavoring that may entice your beardie—and makes a great calcium supplement when ground to a powder. Other brands may also work, but read the ingredients to be sure that they are made of pure calcium carbonate. (Flavorings are okay but not other medicines.)

Multivitamin Supplements

Another type of supplement is the multivitamin supplement. (Usually a multivitamin supplement is actually a multivitamin/multimineral supplement containing an array of different minerals such as iron and zinc.) There is some controversy over this type of supplement because it has been implicated in vitamin overdoses (hypervitaminosis), especially of vitamin A. Choosing a high-quality supplement and using it sparingly will eliminate this hazard.

It is not always easy to tell how good a supplement is; supplement labels are full of unfamiliar and complicated-looking words. There are a few things that can help you make a good choice. First, ask other dragon keepers what they use. Talk to the source of your pet, other hobbyists you may know, and online bearded dragons forums—to name just a few places—and see if you can find a consensus on the best brands. While these different sources are unlikely to agree on one brand, you should notice that two or three brands are consistently recommended. You should also ask your veterinarian for an opinion.

Second, there are a few things to look for on the label. To start with, only use a supplement made specifically for reptiles and amphibians. Vitamins meant for birds, dogs, cats, or other animals are inappropriate for reptiles. Make sure that the label has an expiration date and that the expiration date has not passed. Compare the labels of several supplements; look for the one with the widest variety of vitamins and minerals—it's a good sign if the supplement also includes amino acids. If the supplement

One way to provide calcium supplementation to your dragon is to coat some insects in it, as shown with these king mealworms.

contains calcium and phosphorus, they should be in a 2:1 ratio of calcium to phosphorus. Lastly, the supplement should not contain vitamin A. Instead, it should contain beta carotene, which the dragon's body will convert to vitamin A as needed. Bearded dragons are especially prone to overdoses of vitamin A. Providing beta carotene instead prevents this problem.

How to Use Supplements

Once you have decided on which supplement or supplements to use, you have to get them into your dragon. The simplest way is to sprinkle the powder on his food. Although there is some concern that this will make his food distasteful, it's very rare that a bearded dragon rejects food even if it is covered with vitamin powder.

Many keepers find it best to use supplements on the feeder insects rather than on the fruits and vegetables they offer their lizards. One reason for this is that the veggies are often wet, causing the supplements to clump up and perhaps to break down a bit, rendering them less effective. Another reason is that while bearded dragons may not eat all of their daily veggies, they will almost never leave uneaten insects behind. Applying supplements to the insects ensures that your lizard will get them.

So how do you get vitamins onto an insect? You use a method called dusting (sometimes called "shake-n-bake" for reasons that will become clear shortly). To do this, place a small amount of supplement—maybe half a teaspoon

When Crickets Attack

If your dragon isn't hungry, crickets and other insects wandering around the cage will cause stress and create health hazards by defecating in the food or water bowls or by drowning in the water. Roaming crickets will also get hungry and may attack your beloved pet. Cricket attacks can cause surprisingly serious wounds, and small lizards have been killed by crickets. Prevent this from happening to your dragon by not feeding more insects than your beardie can eat in about ten minutes and by promptly removing any uneaten insects after that time.

or so—in a jar, sandwich bag, or other container. Then drop the number of insects you are going to feed into the container. Gently shake or roll the container around until the insects are covered with supplement. Feed them to your beardie right away, before the supplements get brushed off.

Do not add supplements to your dragon's water. There are several reasons this is a bad idea. It can cause the vitamins to decompose, so he won't actually be getting the full amount.

If you are housing multiple beardies in one enclosure, make sure that each one gets enough food at every feeding.

The supplements can cause bacteria to grow rapidly in the water, creating a possible disease risk. The supplements can also make the water taste bad, so your dragon won't drink it. Lastly, bearded dragons don't drink a lot of water, so putting the supplements into the water may mean that he's not getting enough of them.

How Often to Supplement

How often you give your beardie supplements will depend on his age. Hatchlings and young dragons up to about four months old need calcium supplements daily. They should be given a multivitamin/ multimineral supplement about twice a week. Juvenile beardies between four months and a year old should receive calcium supplements four to five times weekly and multivitamin/ multimineral supplements once a week. Once a beardie is a year old or older, cut back the supplementation so that he receives calcium supplements about three times a week and multivitamin/multimineral supplements once to twice a month. A sickly bearded dragon may need additional supplements, as prescribed by your veterinarian. Breeding females should receive extra calcium supplements about five times weekly.

How to Feed Bearded Dragons

Now that you know what to feed bearded dragons, you must learn how to feed them.

Ratio of Vegetables to Insects

The exact proportion of the diet that should comprise plants versus how much should comprise insects is up for debate. It was once thought that bearded dragons primarily should eat insects and be supplemented with occasional vegetables and fruits. Over the years, the trend among professional breeders and experienced hobbyists has been to recommend higher proportions of vegetables in the diet. Bearded dragons seem to do better when fed more vegetables. Vegetables should make up at least 50 percent of the diet of adult dragons, and 75 percent is probably ideal.

Food Presentation

You will need to feed different types of food in different ways. Fruits and vegetables should be placed in bowls or on plates, which will keep them out of the substrate. You can also attach leafy greens to a screen cage top or prop them up against cage furnishings so that they resemble natural branches. This will give your lizard an opportunity to perform some natural foraging behaviors.

Crickets can just be tossed into the cage for your dragon to hunt down. Most other insects should be placed in a deep bowl to prevent them from escaping before your beardie finds them. It can be difficult to feed roaches to lizards because they are fast and quick to hide. You can solve this problem by feeding roaches individually with forceps or by using a steep-sided glass bowl for those roaches that cannot climb glass. Roaches that escape your dragon right away are likely to be eaten later, but they may also escape the enclosure.

If you feed rodents, feed them directly to your dragon from forceps. This will ensure that your lizard eats the rodent right away before it rots.

Feeding Schedule

How often you feed your bearded dragon depends on his age and general condition. If he is on the thin side or is recovering from an illness, he will need to be fed more often than normal for his age. This is also true for breeding females.

Hatchlings and beardies up to six months old are growing rapidly, and they need plenty of food to fuel that growth. They should have vegetables available at all times, especially if you are housing several hatchlings together.

Calcium and Multivitamin Supplementation Schedule

Dragon's Age	Give Calcium Supplement	Give Multivitamin
hatchling to 4 months old	daily	2 times /week
4 months to 1 year	4–5 times/week	weekly
older than 1 year	3 times/week	1–2 times/month

Plants in a Bearded Dragon Diet

Excellent—Can Be Fed Daily	Good—Can Be Fed Frequently	Acceptable—Can Be Fed Occasionally	Poor—Can Be Fed Rarely if at All
arugula	asparagus	apple	banana
cactus fruit	bell pepper	blueberry	beet and beet greens
cactus pads	blackberry	bok choy	chard
collard greens	borage	broccoli	cucumber
dandelions	chicory	brussels sprouts	grape
endive	cilantro	cabbage	kiwi
escarole	fig	celery leaves	lettuce (all types)
mustard greens	green beans	cherry	parsley
turnip greens	okra	guava	pomegranate
winter squash (e.g., acorn, butternut, Hubbard)	papaya	kale	potato
	pumpkin	kohlrabi	raspberry
	radicchio	leek	spinach
	sweet potato	mango	star fruit
	wheat grass	melons (all types)	tomato
	yam	nectarine	
		peach	
		pear	
		pineapple	
		radish	
		rapini	
		snow pea	
		strawberry	
		watercress	
		zucchini	

If hatchlings get hungry between insect feedings, they will often nibble on the toes and tails of their cagemates, which can result in the loss of a limb or tail or occasionally death. All veggies should be chopped or grated into bite-sized pieces. Feed hatchlings insects two to three times daily. Each hatchling should get about ten appropriately sized insects at each feeding. Do not feed mealworms to hatchlings; they might cause paralysis.

Juvenile dragons between six months and a year of age need a serving of vegetables and appropriately sized insects daily. You may now safely include mealworms and larger insects in the diet. If you wish, you can feed pinky or fuzzy mice to your dragon once a month.

Dragons more than a year old are growing slowly, so they do not need as many feedings as younger lizards. Feed your adult beardie a small bowl of fruits and vegetables each day. Feed him insects every other day. At this age, there are few insects too large for him to eat. You can offer a small mouse once a month, assuming he is not overweight.

How Much to Feed

Young bearded dragons grow at a tremendous rate, so it is hard to overfeed them. You can safely feed them about as much as they will eat. Adult bearded dragons are prone to obesity when kept as pets, so you must more carefully monitor your adult's weight and adjust his food intake accordingly. (See Chapter 5 for more information on obesity.) Vegetables are low in fat, so you can feed these items in large quantities. With insects, feed as many as your bearded dragon can eat in about ten minutes. Remove any uneaten insects after this period.

Water

As creatures of the desert, bearded dragons are adapted to conserve water and to get most of the water they need from their food. However, your lizard should have clean water available at all times. The water bowl should not be very large, because you don't want to raise the humidity in the cage too much. It only needs to be big enough so that there is enough water to last through the whole day. Clean the bowl and add fresh water daily.

Hatchlings up to about three months of age are somewhat prone to dehydration. Provide them water in a *very* shallow container, such as a large jar lid, to prevent drowning. In addition to this, spray them with water from a clean misting bottle once or twice a day.

Chapter 4

A Dragon in
Hand

Most people buy a bearded dragon because beardies
can be handled. They are not aggressive and
adapt easily to handling. However, there is more
to handling your lizard than just picking him up.
There are ways to handle him that will make it safe
and fun for you both. While he's out of his cage for
a handling session, this is a good time to perform
any needed grooming. Dragons require very little
grooming, but performing a little nail trimming
can make handling him more pleasant for you.

Handling

One of the great joys of bearded dragon ownership is that these are lizards that tolerate—and possibly enjoy—being handled. They are normally unafraid of people and seem quite content to come out of their cage and be the center of attention. Here are some do's and don'ts for handling bearded dragons that will keep both you and your lizard safe.

Picking Him up

How you pick up your dragon will depend greatly on his age. If he is a juvenile of less than about four months, you must be very careful handling him and should probably handle him only when necessary. The best way to pick up a young dragon is to use one hand to herd him into the palm of the other. Once in your palm, he is likely to sit there but may move up onto your forearm. If it seems that he is going to take off, you can lightly fold your other hand over him, being careful to put no pressure on his body that could interfere with his breathing.

Older dragons are much more durable. Picking one of these beardies up is as simple as gently sliding your fingers under his midsection and lifting. He'll probably squirm to orient himself so that he is resting

lengthwise on your arm. Once situated, he'll likely be content to sit there as long as you don't move quickly or jerkily.

Always be slow and gentle when picking up your dragon. He will not appreciate being snatched out of his cage or ripped off his branch. This will alarm him, and he may even react as if he were being grabbed by a predator—thrashing, hissing, and biting.

Things Not to Do

Never pick up a bearded dragon by his tail, because it can easily break off. This will cause your lizard pain and will leave a site open for infection. The tail will grow back, but it will be stunted and probably discolored.

Avoid handling him after he's had a meal—it's possible he'll regurgitate if you do. Beardies need high temperatures to digest correctly, and taking him out of his cage with

It's best to allow a young dragon to crawl up onto your palm, rather than picking him up with your hand.

a bellyful of food can cause an upset stomach. Wait a couple of hours after feeding to hold him.

Don't keep your dragon out of his cage for too long. Unless it is really warm in your house, room temperature is too cool for your beardie. He will be soaking up some heat from your body, but overall he'll be cold when he's outside his cage. Put him back in his enclosure if starts to get sluggish or darkens in color. Those are signs that he is too cold. In any case, he shouldn't be out of the cage longer than an hour or so.

Grooming

Bearded dragons require very little in the way of grooming, although you may need to trim your lizard's nails or aid in the shedding process.

Nail Trimming

If you provide your beardie with enough rocks and branches to climb on, his nails will likely stay worn down enough so that you won't have to trim them yourself. Trim his nails only if they are becoming overgrown.

Your beardie's nails are overgrown if they begin to curl under the toe. Note that the nails naturally have a slight curve to them, but the tips should not be under the toe itself or point back toward the body. If not corrected, your dragon could injure himself with the overgrown nail.

It is completely understandable if you are nervous about cutting his nails. A veterinarian will be happy to do it for you if you don't think that you can

FAMILY-FRIENDLY TIP

Children and Handling Lizards

Kids naturally want to pet and handle animals, including bearded dragons. For the most part, this should be encouraged, but you need to ensure the safety of both the lizard and the child. Toddlers and very young children should not be allowed to hold a beardie, but they can safely pet one. Wash the child's hands immediately afterward. You must carefully show an older child how to hold a bearded dragon. Go slowly and calmly, and warn her not to squeeze the lizard. Make sure that she keeps the beardie away from her face—bites are highly unlikely, but take no chances. Explain to the child that she must not put her hands into her mouth and has to wash them right after she's done holding the lizard. One last thing to remember is that you should not allow a child to open the cage and take the beardie out when you are not there to supervise. Depending on the child, you may need to lock the cage. Children handling bearded dragons without adults present is a health hazard to both the child and the lizard.

A Dragon in Hand

Beardies are usually quite content to ride on their owners' shoulders. Be sure to put yours back in his cage before he gets too cold.

do it. Also, a vet can show you how firsthand and answer any questions about the process.

If you are going to trim the nails yourself, buy a good pair of bird or cat claw trimmers. Along with the clippers, get the other supplies ready and within easy reach. You should have a towel in case you need to restrain your dragon, a nail file so that you can smooth out any rough or cracked edges, and some type of blood-stopping agent in case you nick the quick, the blood vessels that supply the nail. (Styptic powder is best, but flour, cornstarch, or a wet tea bag will work.) Having a helper is a good idea too. Once you have all of this together in a work space that is free of clutter, go get your dragon.

Because beardies are so mellow and easy to handle, you may not need to restrain yours for the trimming. This is the best-case scenario—restraint will stress him out. If you go slowly, you may be able to snip the nails without annoying or alarming him. This takes practice. If he gets fidgety after you do a few nails, take a 20-minute break and then trim a few more.

You will only need to trim off the

very tip of the nail. Take off a little at a time; it's better to take off too little than too much. If you trim too deeply, you will hit the quick. That will cause bleeding and some pain. Without panicking, act quickly to stop the bleeding. Press the bleeding end of the toe into the blood-stopping agent. The nail should stop bleeding in a few minutes. After it has stopped, it's a good idea to dab a little antibiotic ointment on the nail to prevent infection. Check the nail a few times over the next couple of hours to make sure that it doesn't start bleeding again—it usually won't, but you can't be too careful. Also, keep an eye on the spot to make sure that it doesn't get infected.

Shedding

Periodically your dragon will shed his skin. Unlike snakes, bearded dragons shed their skin in bits and pieces, not in one continuous piece. Young, rapidly growing dragons shed much more often than adults. Beardies will also shed more frequently if they have external parasites. Some will stop eating during a shed or seem irritated by the process.

Normally, your beardie will not need any help shedding. You will not be helping if you pull pieces off—in fact, you can cause injury. You can mist the cage a few times or give your dragon a supervised soak in 1 or 2 inches (2.5 to 5 cm) of warm water when he's shedding. This will soften the skin and allow it to fall off more easily, but it is not necessary most of the time.

Otherwise, the process will take care of itself.

After the shed, check to make sure that all the skin came off. The toes and tip of the tail are the areas where skin sometimes sticks. If this is the case, soak your dragon in warm water for about 20 minutes. After this, use your fingers to gently rub away the remaining skin.

He Bit Me

Bearded dragons rarely bite people. Bites generally will happen in only three situations: the dragon is very scared or startled, you interrupt him during a territorial display, or you are hand-feeding him. A large beardie can pack quite the bite, and it will hurt. A bite will break the skin but not be able to cause serious injury.

If you're bitten, remain calm. If your dragon is out of his enclosure when the bite occurs, you must first get him back in the cage. After that, wash out the wound with soap and water. It's not a bad idea to use some type of antiseptic, such as peroxide. Dry off the area. Apply a dab of antibiotic ointment and a bandage. Clean and rebandage daily until it's healed.

It's best to avoid handling a beardie when he's puffing up his beard.

Hygiene

All pets carry various bacteria, and some of those bacteria can cause illness in the pet keeper. Bearded dragons are no exception, so you have to practice some commonsense hygiene when handling your dragon and any items from his cage.

Salmonella

Of particular concern when dealing with reptiles is salmonella. Although this illness can be serious, if you practice good hygiene there is less chance of contracting a salmonella infection from your lizard than there is from eating chicken salad at a barbeque. In a healthy person, a salmonella infection (technically called salmonellosis) is like having a really bad stomach flu. The signs are vomiting, diarrhea, abdominal pain and cramping, and fever. Generally, this lasts less than a week and usually does not require medical attention unless dehydration becomes severe or there is blood in the vomit or stool. A salmonella infection can be much more serious for the elderly, young children, and immunocompromised individuals.

Good Hygiene Practices

First and foremost, always wash your hands with soap and water or use hand sanitizer after handling your beardie or any items from his cage. You must also instruct everyone else in the household

The Expert Knows

A Clean Cage Means a Clean Dragon

One way to keep the bacteria on your beardie to a minimum is to keep his cage clean. If he is forced to live in a filthy enclosure, he's going to be exposed to a lot more bacteria than if he's in a clean enclosure. You in turn will also be exposed to more bacteria. Spot clean the cage as needed, and clean the whole substrate regularly. A clean cage is better for both your dragon and you!

After your dragon sheds his skin, check his toes for any bits of skin that didn't drop off.

or anyone who handles your lizard to do the same. Before you wash your hands, make sure that you do not put your hands into your mouth or rub your eyes. When handling your beardie or cleaning his cage, avoid eating, drinking, and smoking. If you allow your children to handle your beardie, be especially vigilant that they do not put their fingers—or the lizard—into their mouths.

Never let your dragon near surfaces used for human food preparation. He should never be allowed on kitchen counters. If you use the sink or bathtub for bathing your beardie, spray it with bleach immediately afterward.

Allow the bleach to soak on the surfaces for at least 15 minutes before rinsing.

When you are washing his food and water bowls, it's best to use the dishwasher because the combination of high heat and steam kills bacteria. If you use the sink, remove all the human food dishes and utensils first. It's a good idea to have a designated dragon sponge or washcloth.

Lastly, as much as you may feel that your beardie is a member of the family, don't kiss him. You are just asking for an infection if you smooch your lizard. Also, do not share food with him or allow him to eat off your plate.

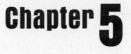

Chapter 5

The Healthy
Dragon

Bearded dragons are hardy reptiles. This is one of the attributes that make them such good pets for novice keepers. A well-cared-for beardie is unlikely to become ill, but nothing is a sure bet. As a responsible dragon keeper, you need to know how to recognize certain problems, how to handle simple issues, and how to get help for the serious stuff.

Reptile Veterinarians

Next to you, your bearded dragon's best friend is his reptile veterinarian. A reptile veterinarian has the specialized training and knowledge to diagnose and treat health problems that are specific to reptiles.

As a whole, reptile keepers do not take their animals in for annual checkups or well visits, and that's a shame. An annual exam allows you and your veterinarian to keep on top of your bearded dragon's health and hopefully catch any illnesses in their early stages when they are most treatable. It's also far better to have an established relationship with a vet if you have an emergency than to be scrambling to find one when your lizard's life is on the line.

Finding a Reptile Veterinarian

Fortunately, veterinarians specializing in the care of reptiles and amphibians have become more common than they were not so long ago. However, finding a herp vet outside a major metropolitan area can still be tricky. There are a number of resources you can access that can help you locate one. One of the first places you can check is the Association of Reptile and Amphibian Veterinarians at www.arav.org. You can search its member directory to see if one has an office near you. Not all good herp veterinarians are members of this organization, however, so you may need to look elsewhere to find one near you.

Word of mouth is an excellent way to find a good veterinarian. You

FAMILY-FRIENDLY TIP

Going to the Vet

When your dragon needs to go to the vet, your child will be curious and may want to come along. Whether you let her is entirely up to you and should be based on her age and maturity. It's probably not a good idea to bring a toddler or very young child with you unless another adult can come to watch her. Keeping a toddler under control while trying to pay attention to what the vet says is just asking to miss important information.

If you take your child to the vet visit, explain what's happening at an age-appropriate level. Tell her that the vet will likely have to restrain your beardie to examine him fully, and this is not hurting him even though he'll probably struggle. It's okay for her to ask the vet questions, but she needs to be quiet while the vet is talking so that you don't miss anything.

If your dragon is gravely ill and the prognosis is poor or if your beardie actually dies, it's best to be honest with your child. Although she will be upset, it's less upsetting if you confront the situation honestly and compassionately.

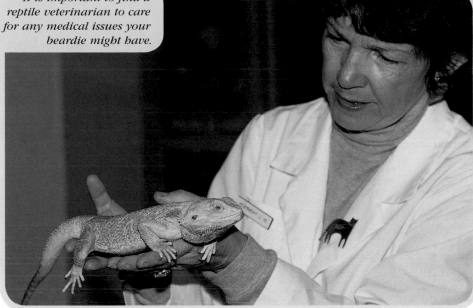

It is important to find a reptile veterinarian to care for any medical issues your beardie might have.

can ask local pet stores and animal shelters which vet treats their reptiles. If you have a herpetological society in the nearby area, the members are sure to know which vets in the area are skilled at reptile medicine. Get recommendations from other herp hobbyists you know.

Once you have a prospective vet, give the office a call and ask a few relevant questions. (If the vet or hospital has a website, you may find the answers there.) You want to find out how long the vet has been treating reptiles and roughly how often he sees reptile patients. You can also ask how often he sees bearded dragons. If you get a good feeling from the phone conversation, make an appointment.

The Well Visit

Make an appointment to see your vet soon after you acquire your beardie. The vast majority of bearded dragons are healthy when they are sold, but it's best to make certain. Also, some pet stores and other vendors may not honor a health guarantee on the beardie if you don't take him to the vet's within a certain period.

At this first visit, the vet will take a complete history of your dragon, asking you detailed questions about all aspects of his care. She will likely make suggestions for areas of care that you can improve on or may just confirm that you are doing a good job. She will weigh your dragon and look him over thoroughly, including the inside of his mouth and possibly

Take your dragon to the vet's for a well visit soon after you acquire him.

in his vent. If anything is amiss, she'll order or perform needed tests, take an X-ray, and/or draw some blood for analysis.

Brumation

Wild bearded dragons are subject to seasonal changes of temperature, hours of daylight, and humidity. To survive the winters when temperatures are low and food is less plentiful, the dragons dig a deep burrow and hole up there, entering a state of torpor. This is similar to hibernation in mammals, but in reptiles, the process is referred to as "brumation." (There is some debate about how correct this term is and how similar the process is to that which mammals go through, but for our purposes, brumation is fine.) This

is not a deep sleep, just a reduction in activity and metabolism that enables beardies to survive until the bountiful days of spring return. Even during seasonal brumation, beardies may emerge from their burrows on particularly warm days and then return when the temperature falls again.

Your dragon will likely not experience a dramatic change of seasons because you'll be providing high temperatures, bright light, and plentiful food all year round. However, it's difficult to ignore millions of years of evolutionary adaptation. Some pet bearded dragons will still become sluggish during the winter. This winter can be the same as your winter, or your dragon may be on the seasonal cycles of "down under," where winter runs from June to September. You can also stimulate your beardie to enter brumation by reducing temperatures and/or lighting. You probably won't be doing this on purpose, but it could happen if you aren't keeping track of the temperatures in his cage. However, if you want to breed your bearded dragons, putting them through a brumation period is often necessary.

How Dragons Brumate

If your dragon starts becoming less and less active and eating less food, he could be starting brumation. Note that juvenile beardies rarely brumate on their own; usually only adults enter brumation. If your bearded dragon is getting ready to brumate, he is likely to spend less time basking—this is a key sign because a sick bearded dragon will usually bask more. He will spend more time in the cooler areas of his cage and more time in his hide box. He will probably burrow down into his substrate and not come out even when fed.

Just before fully entering brumation, your dragon will stop eating completely and empty out his digestive tract (i.e., poop). While brumating, a dragon won't be digesting, so any food left inside will rot and make him sick. Hence, he'll stop eating some time before fully going torpid. After this, he'll hole up someplace cool and dark and go into a deep sleep.

Some dragons stay in this sleep for two to three months without waking up at all (and you may not be able to wake him up even if you try). Others will just take long naps and be inactive and sluggish when awake. Each beardie is an individual. Many will not brumate at all or brumate only some years and not others. When his body tells him it's time to wake up and be active, he'll start resting less and less and will begin eating.

Give Me Fever

Humans and other warm-blooded animals get fevers when they are ill because the rise in body temperature actually helps fight off an infection. Perhaps surprisingly, reptiles also get fevers. The difference is that they create their own fevers with behavior. A reptile that is feeling ill will often keep himself as warm as he can. He may bask for far longer periods and at higher temperatures than normal.

You can use this knowledge to help your beardie should he ever become sick. You should raise the temperature at the basking spot by up to 10°F (5.5°C). Don't raise the temperature of the cool end of the cage too much, because you want to give him the opportunity to cool down if he wants to. While your dragon is sick, keep the nighttime temperatures elevated a bit by using a ceramic heat emitter. Raising the temperature slightly is especially effective at helping fight off respiratory infections.

What You Need to Do

If your dragon starts brumating, you really can't stop him. There are some things you can do to make sure that he stays healthy during his long winter's nap. The first and most important thing to do is schedule a vet appointment as soon as you can. You want to make sure that he's in top condition before he really goes into torpor. He's going to be spending several weeks not eating, so his body needs to be able to do this. It's especially important that he not have any parasites at this time. His immune system will not be working at its best, so any untreated parasites he has are likely to explode in population during brumation. If your beardie has a clean bill of health, let him do his thing and don't worry.

You will need to provide a suitable spot for him to sleep in. A dark hide box that is just large enough to fit your dragon will work well. Beardies like to brumate in fairly small spaces, so don't make it too big. If you wish, you can simulate the seasonal changes in lighting by reducing the time his lights are on to as little as eight hours each day. When brumation is over, gradually

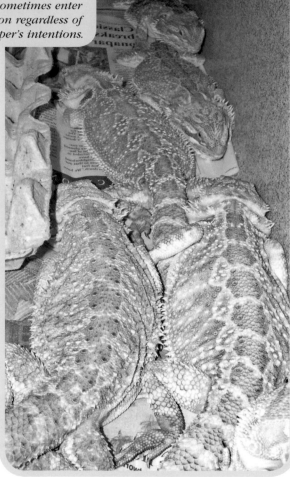

A group of brumating dragons at a breeder's facility. Beardies will sometimes enter brumation regardless of their keeper's intentions.

increase the photoperiod to the normal 12 to 14 hours. You can also reduce the temperature somewhat. If he wakes up and wanders around the cage, you can offer him some food, but don't be surprised if he doesn't eat.

Check on your dragon periodically to make sure that he's still healthy. Do this weekly. If he's one of the lizards that wakes up occasionally, this is a perfect time to give him a once-over and weigh him. Beardies will lose only a few grams over the course of brumation. You also have to make sure that he stays hydrated during brumation. To do this, take him out of his cage and put him in a container with about 1 inch (2.5 cm) of warm water in the bottom. Let him sit in the water for 15 minutes or so. Watch him carefully; he may not actually wake and could drown while sleeping. He may or may not drink—either is okay. After the 15 minutes, dry him off and put him back into his hide box.

After Brumation

When your beardie comes out of brumation, it may take a few days to a couple of weeks for him to return to being his old self. He may also not eat for several days. Once he's up and eating, he may start to display territorial and mating behavior. You'll see lots of head bobbing and beard flaring. If your beardie is a female, be aware that brumation often stimulates egg development, even if you have no male.

Egg Binding

When a female beardie becomes gravid (pregnant with eggs), she is sometimes unable to lay those eggs. She might retain them in her body, where they can rupture and cause infection or become overly calcified and injure her reproductive tract. This condition is called egg binding, or dystocia, more scientifically speaking. Although you may never intend to breed your beardie, she may still suffer from egg binding. Female dragons will sometimes produce eggs even when there is no male present. These eggs will be infertile, but

Female beardie digging a nest in her nesting box. Even without a male present, a female dragon will sometimes develop eggs.

Collecting a Sample

When you take your bearded dragon to the vet, use plain paper towels or newspaper to line the bottom of the carrier. This will allow the vet to get a good look at any droppings your beardie leaves. She can get some insight into your dragon's health status with just a quick look at the droppings.

your dragon still needs to lay them as if they could hatch into little beardies.

There are many causes of egg binding. Sometimes an egg forms that is too large to fit through the oviduct. An egg can be misshapen and block the passage. Nutritional problems can also contribute to egg binding. And if a female does not have a suitable nesting site, she may refuse to lay the eggs; when the eggs are retained too long, they become overcalcified and get stuck in the oviduct.

In the late stages of egg development, your female's abdomen will enlarge and take on a lumpy appearance. These are the outlines of the eggs inside her. If she is carrying a large clutch of eggs, it may look as if she swallowed a bunch of marbles.

When she is ready to lay the eggs, she will start digging a nest, so provide her with a good nesting site. A deep pan or tub filled with at least 8 inches (20.3 cm) of moist sand or vermiculite makes a good site. Put this in the female's cage, and make sure that she can get in and out of it easily. If a female has been actively digging, she'll usually lay within two days of being offered a nesting site. You'll know that she laid her eggs because she will appear flabby or deflated. Feed her heavily for the next few weeks, and give her some extra calcium supplementation.

If your female dragon does not lay her eggs within a few days of being given the nesting box, it is possible she is egg bound. However, the time it takes to lay eggs varies greatly among different females. If yours is acting healthy, it's not time to panic yet. Keep the nesting box in her cage and let her do her thing. If she becomes lethargic, depressed, or nonresponsive, take her to your

Slightly raising the temperature at your dragon's basking site can help him recover from respiratory and other infections.

veterinarian immediately—she is an egg-bound dragon. The vet will likely x-ray your dragon to get a better look at what's going on in her oviduct and treat according to what he sees. Medication and surgery are two possible treatments.

Unfortunately, there is no definite way to prevent egg binding, short of having a female dragon spayed—yes, a herp veterinarian can do this, although it isn't common. Keeping your female in top condition and giving her a nest site when she needs one are the only things you can do. Some female dragons just seem prone to this condition; others may suffer from it once and never again.

Impaction

Gut impactions occur when a bit of indigestible matter gets stuck in the digestive tract of a bearded dragon. Sadly, this life-threatening condition is not uncommon. Housing bearded dragons on inappropriate substrates is the most frequent cause of impaction. Other possible causes include basking site temperatures that are too low and feeding insects that are too large. (Mealworms and superworms are the most common offenders.)

The first sign that your dragon is impacted will usually be constipation. If he hasn't passed droppings in two to three days, he is likely constipated (assuming he has been eating). In addition to constipation, a gut-impacted beardie is often sluggish and just won't seem to be himself. He may vomit. In serious cases—frequent in hatchlings suffering from gut impaction—the hind limbs may become paralyzed.

If you suspect that your beardie is suffering from a gut impaction, make a vet appointment as soon as possible. The vet will likely give your dragon an enema, but severe cases may require surgery.

You can help resolve the impaction yourself by soaking him in warm shallow water and gently massaging his abdomen in the direction of his vent. Some keepers report success in relieving impaction by giving their beardies a few drops of vegetable oil orally before the bathing and massage. Even if your lizard passes the impacting material, you should keep

your vet appointment to make sure that all of it was eliminated and that it caused no other complications. Until your veterinarian tells you otherwise, it may be a good idea to switch to a newspaper or paper towel substrate.

Infectious Diseases

When kept in the proper conditions, fed an excellent diet, and kept free from undue stress, bearded dragons rarely contract infections. It is almost always some lapse in the husbandry of these lizards that opens the door for bacterial and fungal infections.

Remember that beardies don't show signs of illness until they are very sick. If you think that your dragon seems ill, take him to the vet sooner rather than later. He will stand the best chance for total recovery if you get him medical attention early.

Veterinarians treat most infections with oral antibiotics and will show you how to administer these to your lizard if necessary.

The signs of infections vary depending on the type of organism causing the infection, its severity, and the location. In general, suspect that your dragon has an infection if you notice any of the following: abnormal droppings; discharge coming from the eyes, nostrils, or vent; discoloration anywhere on the body; a dark gray color over the entire body; redness or swelling anywhere on the body; refusing to eat; sluggishness; or vomiting. Two infections that a keeper should know about are mouth rot and respiratory infections.

Mouth Rot

Mouth rot (more properly called stomatitis) is just as nasty as it sounds. It's an infection of the gums that causes severe inflammation culminating in tooth loss and death of bone tissue. Severe cases can be fatal. This is most commonly seen in lizards that are kept too cool, fed an inadequate diet, and enclosed in filthy cages. Early signs include redness of the gums or lining of the mouth (as opposed to healthy pinkness) and cheesy deposits around the teeth. If allowed to progress, the cheesy deposits will get larger, teeth will fall out, there will be a foul odor coming from the area, and the jaw may become distorted. Also, the dragon will probably stop eating because his mouth hurts too much.

If you suspect that your beardie has mouth rot, seek veterinary care. The vet will clean out that area of the mouth, prescribe antibiotics, and probably give you some type of

Signs That Your Beardie Is Sick

It's important to know how to spot a potential illness or injury in your beardie. The sooner you address the problem, the more likely he is to recover. It's also important to know what's normal for your beardie. If he is acting abnormally in any way, there is a chance he could be ill. Some signs to look out for include:

- abnormal droppings (unusually stinky, odd color, presence of worms, etc.)
- abnormally inactive
- cheesy material in mouth
- discolored patches on skin
- dragging a limb
- refusing food
- sudden weight loss
- vomiting
- wheezing or gurgling noises when breathing

antiseptic oral cleanser. She will also likely go over your care techniques to see if there is any area that you should improve to prevent a recurrence.

Respiratory Infection

Bearded dragons who are kept too

cool or too humid often develop respiratory infections. These can also be a complication of mouth rot. Signs are similar to those in people: discharge from the nose, sneezing, wheezing, and lack of energy. A dragon with a respiratory infection will usually stay in the hottest part of his cage. If your beardie shows any of these signs, seek veterinary care. You should also raise the temperatures of the basking site by about 10°F (5.5°C) and provide some supplemental nighttime heating.

Injuries

The sad truth about bearded dragon injuries is that almost all of them could've been prevented by the keeper. It is usually some type of negligence on the keeper's part that causes a dragon to become hurt. The most common types of injuries are burns, wounds caused by other dragons, and injuries related to being dropped. Injuries caused by falling or shifting cage furnishings are also common. (See Chapter 2.)

Burns

Inappropriate housing is the most common cause of burns—the dragon is able to get too close to his heat lamp. Sometimes a faulty heating device is to blame. To prevent both types of burns, set up the cage in such a way that your beardie cannot get too close to the light, and monitor the cage temperatures daily. Be aware that the screen top directly beneath a heat lamp may also get hot enough to cause a burn.

Burns are quite serious for bearded dragons and other small pets. If your dragon suffers a burn—no matter how minor—take him to the vet for treatment. If you cannot get to the vet right away, wash the area with cool clean water and dab a little

A bearded dragon's mouth normally has a yellowish tint on the roof and tongue.

This female dragon lost her foot to an overly aggressive male. Although many keepers house their dragons together, it is risky.

antibiotic ointment or pure aloe vera (directly from the plant is best) on the site of the burn. The veterinarian will assess the wound and perform initial treatment but is likely to give you instructions for at-home care. Follow them precisely. Switching to a newspaper, paper towel, or cage liner for substrate until the burn heals is a good idea because sand may get stuck in the burn and cause further complications.

Falling Injuries

Injuries related to being dropped or falling can be quite complicated and often require veterinary treatment. If your dragon falls from a substantial height, seek emergency care, especially if he behaves in any way abnormally after the fall. The best way to prevent such accidents is to hold him correctly and to keep a careful eye on him when he is out of his cage. (See Chapter 4.)

Wounds

Open wounds on a bearded dragon are most frequently caused by cagemates. Even bearded dragons who have seemed the best of friends for years can turn on each other without warning. This is especially true of males. Obviously, the best way to prevent this type of wound is to house each beardie in his own cage. Another common cause of wounds is sharp or pointy cage furnishings. Carefully inspect all objects for safety before placing them into your dragon's enclosure.

Most keepers can treat small wounds themselves. Any wound that is deep, that won't stop bleeding, or that causes some disability must be treated by a veterinarian as soon as possible. Wounds caused by other dragons almost always require veterinary attention. To treat a minor wound, clean it out with water or sterile saline. Dab a bit of antibiotic ointment on the wound once a day until it is fully closed.

Nutritional Illnesses

Unfortunately, nutritional problems are quite common in bearded dragons and other pet reptiles. If you follow the diet laid out in Chapter 3, your beardie should not suffer from any dietary problems. However, it is in your lizard's best interest if you understand and learn to recognize diet-caused illnesses.

Metabolic Bone Disease

Metabolic bone disease (MBD) is a catchall term for a variety of ailments all stemming from either a lack of calcium or lack of vitamin D. Too much phosphorus in the diet also contributes. This is one of the most commonly seen problems in bearded dragons, and it is totally preventable. If you provide your dragon with an excellent diet (including appropriate calcium supplementation) and the proper UV lighting, there is almost no chance he will get MBD.

The signs of MBD are similar to

Hatchling dragons are more prone to MBD and other nutritional problems than adults are.

those of rickets in humans. The bones become weak and flexible, so the limbs become bent or curved. The jaw is often one of the first bones affected, becoming soft and bending outwardly. It is for this reason that MBD is sometimes called "rubber jaw." Deformities of the spine are also common. If not corrected, the dragon will begin to have tremors and spasms and spontaneous bone fractures. Movements become painful—or even impossible due to joint deformities—

so beardies with severe MBD may not move around much. If your beardie shows any hint of having MBD, seek veterinary treatment. The vet will likely take X-rays and draw some blood for testing. If MBD is the issue, the vet may give calcium injections and/or prescribe oral calcium supplements. The vet will surely discuss your dragon's care with you to address the cause of the MBD.

Vitamin A Toxicity

When kept as pets, bearded dragons tend to be especially sensitive to having too much vitamin A in their diets. Overdosing on vitamin A causes vitamin A toxicity, also called hypervitaminosis A. Usually this is caused by overusing vitamin supplements. Supplement only as recommended in Chapter 3 or as directed by your veterinarian. Also, using a supplement that has beta carotene instead of vitamin A goes a long way toward preventing this problem.

The signs of vitamin A toxicity include throat swelling, bloating, and sluggishness. If your dragon exhibits these signs, discontinue supplementation and seek veterinary care.

Obesity is common in pet bearded dragons because many keepers overfeed them.

97

Obesity

Bearded dragons really love to eat, and it's fun to feed them. This can rapidly lead to having them gaining too much weight and becoming obese. As with humans, obese beardies are

The Healthy Dragon

more prone to a host of other health problems, such as egg binding and fatty liver disease, and have shortened life spans. Besides feeding beardies too much, feeding them too many insects or rodents and not enough vegetables contributes to obesity. Stick to the recommended diet of varied greens and other vegetables daily, insects every other day, and rodents occasionally or not at all.

The best way to see whether your beardie is becoming overweight is to weigh him regularly. You'll need a scale that weighs in grams because those units are the most accurate when weighing small animals such as bearded dragons. An adult beardie should weigh between 300 and 500 grams, depending on his size. What's more important than the actual weight is the change in weight. If your fully grown dragon weighs 430 grams at one weighing, 440 the next, and 475 the next, you are probably overfeeding. Besides weighing him, look at your dragon. If his belly is dragging the ground when he walks, he is overweight.

If you find yourself with a portly beardie, cut back on feeding insects and rodents. Eliminate rodents from the diet altogether, and feed only half the number of insects at each feeding as you normally would. Skip feeding him entirely for one day each week. Also, make sure that the cage is large enough for him to move around, and let him out for supervised exercise as much as you can. Take your obese dragon to the vet for further advice on safely reducing his weight and to make sure

Stress—the Hidden Illness

Bearded dragons suffer from stress when conditions in their habitat are not appropriate. Temperatures that are too cool, insufficient lighting, cramped quarters, and overly humid enclosures all cause stress. There are also less easily noticed sources of stress for a pet bearded dragon. Such things such as being kept in a room that is brightly lit even at night, loud noises, being harassed by cagemates, young kids banging on the cage walls, moving to a new cage, and being handled too frequently all cause stress.

Stress is a big deal because it suppresses the immune system and affects hormone secretion. Long-term stress will eventually make your bearded dragon sick. At the very least, it predisposes him to infections as his immune system stops functioning correctly. As a responsible dragon keeper, you should do everything you can to minimize the stress your beardie experiences.

that his weight has not caused other health problems.

Parasites

Parasites are organisms that live on or inside another organism and feed on that organism, or in the case of many gastrointestinal parasites, on the food that organism ingests. In general, parasites can be divided into two types: external and internal. External parasites live on the skin and usually feed by sucking blood. Internal parasites live inside the host animal. Parasites are extremely common in nature, and almost every animal has some number of parasites. They tend to be most numerous on wild-caught reptiles, but they are seen in captive-bred reptiles, including bearded dragons, as well.

If your bearded dragon contracts any form of parasite, you should make some changes to your housing and maintenance routine until the parasite is eliminated. Start by getting rid of the substrate and using newspaper or paper towels. These substrates are easy to replace daily, which you will now be doing, and do not harbor parasites as easily as most other substrates. Remove any wooden, porous, or organic objects from the cage. They should be thrown away, although you can try to disinfect certain objects. Replace furnishings with easily cleaned alternatives, and furnish the cage with the bare minimum—a single climbing branch and a hide box.

Mites

Mites are one of the most commonly seen health problems in pet reptiles. The best way to think of mites is as the fleas of reptiles. They are tiny bloodsucking parasites that infest their hosts in tremendous numbers, and they reproduce rapidly, so just a few mites become thousands of mites in no time. These insidious parasites drain the blood of your pet, weakening him and compromising his health. Although there has been no documented evidence that mites can spread other diseases, the possibility certainly exists. If you notice mites, you must eliminate them immediately. Note that the mites that infest bearded dragons and other reptiles will feed only on these animals. They do not

Mites often hide in the folds of skin around a bearded dragon's eyes.

This beardie is very thin, a common sign of worms and other digestive parasites.

pose a danger to humans or to other nonreptilian pets.

Like many other health issues, mites more frequently turn up on wild-caught reptiles than on captive-bred ones. However, that does not mean that your beardie is safe from these bloodsuckers. They spread easily from one reptile to another, so your beardie could have gotten them from other reptiles housed at the same pet store or breeder's facility. You could even give them to your dragon! Mites could hitch a ride on you if you handle infested reptiles at a pet store or herp expo. Always clean your hands after handling reptiles.

Mites are often difficult to spot.

They are tiny—about the size of ground pepper. Often brown or gray, they blend in with a dragon and his habitat. They usually go unnoticed until you find small dots crawling on you after handling your dragon. This is a certain sign that your lizard has mites. Another sign is small, dark, dirt-like particles at the bottom of your beardie's water bowl; these particles are drowned mites. If you see this, you likely have mites. To make certain, take a damp white paper towel and wipe your beardie's skin with it. Wipe all over, especially the places mites like to hide: the corners of the mouth, the folds of skin near the vent, around the eyelids, and the places where the limbs meet the body. Look closely at the paper towel afterward. If you see any small moving dots, your dragon has mites.

There are a number of ways to get rid of mites. While there are numerous home remedies that you can find on the Internet, a veterinarian can provide you with an oral medication or a miticidal spray that will definitely work. The active ingredient is usually ivermectin, a widely prescribed antiparisitic medication. Note that if you keep turtles or tortoises, ivermectin is deadly to them. Keep it far away from these animals. Follow your veterinarian's instructions exactly when using prescribed mite treatments.

Mite sprays sold by pet stores are not always effective. Note that mites are resilient, pernicious creatures, and you may need to treat for them several times before your beardie is free of them.

An old treatment for mites was to use insect-killing pesticide strips with the active ingredient Vapona or dichlorvos; they are usually called "no-pest strips." However, there is quite a bit of evidence that these strips can cause injury in

herps, and unless carefully used, can even kill reptiles. Do not use these strips to treat mites.

Worms and Other Internal Parasites

Worms and other internal parasites are extremely common in wild-caught reptiles, but they are less common in bearded dragons and other captive-bred herps. Beardies do get worms and other internal parasites occasionally, usually from some type of cross-contamination, such as putting them into a cage that held other herps and that wasn't properly cleaned beforehand. If you keep other herps besides your dragon, be careful that you don't accidentally pass any parasites from one to the other. Wash your hands in between handling the herps or their cage furnishings, and don't let them come into contact with one another. Make sure that any new herps—especially wild-caught ones—are quarantined far away from your established healthy ones.

Another way beardies can get worms is by feeding them insects that you catch outdoors.

If your dragon has worms, they will often be visible in the feces; other internal parasites are too small to be seen. One of the most telling signs of parasitic infection is changes to the droppings. They may be runny, especially odoriferous, bloody, or oddly colored. (This can also be caused by feeding some colorful foods; for example, feeding beets will cause reddish feces.) Other signs include loss of appetite, bloating, vomiting, constipation, weight loss, and sluggishness. If you suspect that your dragon has parasites, you will need to take him to the vet. Parasites are normally treated with oral medication, but this varies with the type of parasite involved.

Coccidia

One type of digestive parasite, coccidia, is so common in beardies that it is considered normal for them to have it. These protozoans generally do not harm a dragon unless he is suffering from long-term stress, is kept in filthy conditions, or contracts another illness. At such times, the number of coccidia in the lizard's gut explodes in number and begins to affect his health. Signs of a coccidian infestation include diarrhea, weight loss, and dehydration. This condition seems to cause

abdominal pain as well. As with any other digestive parasite, veterinary attention is required for coccidia.

Note that coccidia are resistant to bleach but are killed by ammonia. Use a 10 percent solution in water and allow the ammonia to sit on any surfaces that need disinfection for 30 minutes.

Cryptosporidiosis

A particularly dreadful intestinal parasite is *Cryptosporidium*, and infection with this organism causes a disease called cryptosporidiosis, or "crypto" as it is known by most herp keepers. While it is not as common in bearded dragons as it is in leopard geckos, it infects beardies with some frequency. Keepers need to be especially concerned with crypto because humans can contract it through contact with the feces of infected herps.

The Expert Knows

Check the Temperatures

Cool temperatures can cause a bearded dragon to become sluggish and refuse food. If your beardie exhibits these signs or just appears a bit off, check the cage temperatures before you become too concerned. There is a chance that your beardie is just too cold. If so, fix the temperature issue and he should be back to normal in a couple of hours.

Wash your hands after visiting a pet store or herp expo to avoid bringing an illness home to your dragon.

Although unpleasant, crypto infection in healthy humans goes away by itself in about two weeks. As with coccidia, ammonia is the best disinfectant for killing crypto on surfaces.

The signs of crypto are similar to those caused by other digestive parasites. Additionally, it may also cause swelling of the abdomen. This disease is often fatal to reptiles. One terrible attribute of crypto is that it may cause no symptoms at all for a long time, and during that time, the infected beardie can spread the parasite to other animals.

It is difficult to diagnose crypto with certainty. There is no cure for this disease, although infected beardies can be given treatment that will extend their life spans and quality of life. However, because it is very infectious and eventually fatal, most veterinarians recommend that herps suffering from crypto be humanely euthanized.

Resources

Veterinary Resources

Association of Reptile and Amphibian Veterinarians (ARAV)
P.O. Box 605
Chester Heights, PA 19017
Phone: 610-358-9530
Fax: 610-892-4813
E-mail: ARAVETS@aol.com
www.arav.org

Herp Vet Connection
www.herpvetconnection.com

Herpetological Societies

Amphibian, Reptile, and Insect Association
23 Windmill Rd.
Irthlingsborough
Wellingborough NN9 5RJ
England
www.arianorthampton.com/page2.htm

British Herpetological Society
11 Strathmore Place
Montrose, Angus
DD10 8LQ
United Kingdom
www.thebhs.org

Center for North American Herpetology
www.cnah.org

Chicago Herpetological Society
Phone: (312) 409-4456
www.chicagoherp.org

International Herpetological Society
8 Buxton Lane
Frizinghall, Bradford
W. Yorks, BD9 4LP
England
Telephone: 01-274-548342
E-mail: ihsnewsletter@yahoo.co.uk

Kansas Herpetological Society
Phone: (785) 272-1076)
www.ukans.edu/~khs

League of Florida Herpetological Societies
www.jaxherp.tripod.com/league.htm

Nebraska Herpetological Society
www.nebherp.org

Northern Ohio Association of Herpetologists (N.O.A.H.)
NOAH, Department of Biology
Case Western Reserve University
Cleveland, OH 44106-7080
www.noahonline.info/site_down

San Diego Herpetological Society
PO Box 503835
San Diego CA 92150
E-mail: sdhs@sdherpsociety.org
www.sdherpsociety.org

Western New York Herpetological
Society
www.wnyherp.org/index.php

Rescue and Adoption Services

Colorado Reptile Humane Society
www.corhs.org/index.html

Melissa Kaplan's herp rescue
directory
www.anapsid.org/societies/

National Amphibian and Reptile
Rescue Alliance (NARRA)
www.reptilerescuealliance.org/

New England Amphibian and
Reptile Rescue (NEARR)
www.reptilerescue.net/

Petfinder
www.petfinder.com

Reptile Rescue League
www.reptilerescueleague.org/

VA Reptile Rescue
www.vareptilerescue.org/

Information Sources

Bearded Dragon Care
www.beardeddragoncare.net

Bearded Dragon Custom Cage
Design
//708designs.netfirms.com/
customcage/customcage.htm

BeardedDragon.org
www.beardeddragon.org

Building a Bearded Dragon
Enclosure
www.freewebs.com/
crossfireenclosures/

Herp Station
www.petstation.com/herps.html

International Reptile Conservation
Foundation
www.IRCF.org

Kingsnake.com
www.kingsnake.com

Lizard-Landscapes.com
www.lizard-landscapes.com

The Lizard Wizard
www.thelizardwizard.co.uk/care_
guides.htm

Melissa Kaplan's Herp Care Collection:
Dragons Down Under
www.anapsid.org/bearded.html

The Reptile Forums
www.reptileforums.com

Reptile Rooms
www.reptilerooms.com

Tosney's Bearded Dragon Care
www.bio.miami.edu/ktosney/file/BDcare.html

UK Bearded Dragons
www.ukbeardeddragons.co.uk

Books

Hellweg, Michael R. *Raising Live Foods.* TFH Publications, Inc.

Langerwerf, Bert. *Water Dragons.* TFH Publications, Inc.

Purser, Philip. *Bearded Dragons.* TFH Publications, Inc.

Purser, Philip. *Insect-Eating Lizards.* TFH Publications, Inc.

Purser, Philip. *Natural Terrariums.* TFH Publications, Inc

Sprackland, Robert G. *Giant Lizards, 2nd Edition.* TFH Publications, Inc.

Sprackland, Robert G. *Guide to Lizards.* TFH Publications, Inc.

Taylor, John F. *Uromastyx.* TFH Publications, Inc.

Magazines

HerpDigest
www.herpdigest.org

Reptiles
P.O. Box 6050
Mission Viejo, CA 92690
www.reptilechannel.com/rmrc_portal.aspx

Reptilia
Bisbe Urquinaona, 34
08860 Castelldefels
Barcelona
Spain
www.reptilia.net

Resources

Index

Boldfaced numbers indicate illustrations.

About the Author

Thomas Mazorlig has a BS in biology from Cornell University. He was the editor of *Reptile and Amphibian Hobbyist* magazine and currently edits the reptile, amphibian, and bird books at TFH Publications. Tom has kept a wide variety of reptile species, and he bred bearded dragons, chameleons, and colubrid snakes for many years. He lives in South Amboy, New Jersey, with his partner, a cat, four snakes, and a small herd of tortoises.

Photo Credits

501room (from Shutterstock): 55
Andre Goosen Photography: 73
Yuri Arcurs (from Shutterstock): 62
Abraham Badenhorst (from Shutterstock): 42
Joan Balzarini: 85, 86
Heather Barr (from Shutterstock): 9 (bottom)
R. D. Bartlett: 3
Adam Black: 88, 100
BMCL (from Shutterstock): 38
Allen Both: 17
Alex James Bramwell (from Shutterstock): 47
Annie Mitchell Burge (from Shutterstock): 18
Maynard Case (from Shutterstock): 104, back cover (bottom)
Steve Collender (from Shutterstock): 34, 40, 56, 60, 81, 99, 103, 110
Cre8tive Images (from Shutterstock): 8
Jan de Wild (from Shutterstock): 101
James DeBoer (from Shutterstock): 97
fivespots (from Shutterstock): 12, 43, front cover, back cover (top)
Isabelle Francais: 11, 20, 22, 24, 25, 45, 48, 50, 52, 57, 70, 74, 80, 89

Paul Freed: 7
James E. Gerholdt: 59
Lijuan Guo (from Shutterstock): 90, 109
Kimberly Hall (from Shutterstock): 30
irin-k (from Shutterstock): 91
Mark James (from Shutterstock): 33
Adrian T. Jones (from Shutterstock): 66
Julie Keen (from Shutterstock): 92
Cynthia Kidwell (from Shutterstock): 13
Robert King (from Shutterstock): 6
K.L. Kohn (from Shutterstock): 63
Kirill Kuzminych (from Shutterstock): 27
MalcolmC (from Shutterstock): 78
Marietjie (from Shutterstock): 9 (top)
G. and C. Merker: 15, 82, 96, back cover (bottom center)
Christian Musat (from Shutterstock): 36
Pixel Memoirs (from Shutterstock): 76
Mark Smith: 65
Vinicius Tupinamba (from Shutterstock): 72
John C. Tyson: 10
Sandra van der Steen (from Shutterstock): 4, 31, back cover (top center)
Maleta M. Walls: 28, 53, 95
Ashley Whitworth (from Shutterstock): 94
Feng Yu (from Shutterstock): 23